Rain Forests
and
Cloud Forests

"Come with me, sir, come! A flower, very large, beautiful, wonderful!"

The Malaysian guide bounded down the elephant path to tell Dr. Joseph Arnold of his discovery. Dr. Arnold immediately followed him one hundred yards into the dense, wet Sumatran rain forest. Among some low lianas a truly astonishing sight met his eyes: growing close to the ground was a reddish brown mottled flower the size of a large washtub, fully three feet across! Dr. Arnold sent for the leader of the expedition, Sir Thomas Stamford Raffles, and together they admired the flower.

"My first impulse was to cut it up and carry it to the hut." Arnold wrote to a friend in London of his experience:

> I therefore seized the Malay's parang (a sort of instrument like a woodman's chopping hook), and finding that the flower sprang from a small root which ran horizontally (about as large as two fingers, or a little more), I soon detached it and removed it to our hut. To tell you the truth, had I been alone, and had there been no witnesses, I should I think have been fearful of mentioning the dimensions of this flower, so much does it exceed every flower I have ever seen or heard of; but I had Sir Stamford and Lady Raffles with me, who . . . are able to testify as to the truth. . . .
>
> Now for the dimensions, which are the most astonishing part of the flower. It measured a full yard across; the petals, which were subrotund, being twelve inches from the base to the apex, and it being about a foot from the insertion of the one petal to the opposite one.

The discovery in 1818 of the "great flower," which weighed fifteen pounds and held six quarts of water in the nectaries, created keen interest in scientific circles in London, and the press reported the find at great length. Later, the flower was named *Rafflesia arnoldi.*

The alarm clock rang in the dead of night. Outside it was pitch black. Just yesterday I had arrived in Sumatra at the invitation of Dr. Nitza Arbi of the University of Padang. I intended to film the gigantic *Rafflesia,* hoping to catch its opening in time-lapse motion picture and document its pollination and dispersal of seeds by animals. This morning we wanted to get an early start to look for the four sites where *Rafflesia* was known to have existed.

We started out with flashlights along the dark pathway. After an hour's walk, the first golden glow of dawn illuminated the horizon over the magnificent Sianok Canyon in central Sumatra. Beneath us appeared the lush green rain-forest valley draped in a soft veil of silent mist, penetrated only by the tops of the tallest trees. Just before dawn the rain forest was at its most mysterious; it was a dream landscape.

The trip turned out to be even more interesting than I imagined, but not in the way I had hoped. Instead of hiking through a thick, damp rain forest, we passed small villages and ricefield after ricefield, where nearly every tree had been cut down. When we finally arrived at the site of Sir Stamford Raffles's discovery, we crisscrossed the area at

Photographing the Rain Forest
by Kjell B. Sandved

Left. *Photographer Kjell Sandved explores life in the Amazon rain forest with his camera. The branches of the trees are covered with epiphytes. The pineapplelike leaves are those of bromeliads.*

Following pages. *Fortunately, the sole remaining known location of the world's largest flower,* Rafflesia arnoldi, *has been protected. However,* little *control is exercised and visitors are allowed to trample on developing buds. The flower illustrated was thirty inches (76 cm) in diameter with petals an inch thick. The flower lasts only a few days and issues a fetid smell that attracts flies as pollinators.*

Page 22. *Sandved photographs insects along the Amazonas River in Tingo María, Peru. The biting insects are not visible here!*

length without finding any buds of the *Rafflesia* flower.

When we learned that the second forest reserve where *Rafflesia* had been known to exist was inaccessible because of flooding, we headed toward the third area. Here we were dismayed to find that most of the land had been bulldozed —a foreign company was building a road up the mountainside. All we could find were a few rotting *Rafflesia* buds at the periphery of the site. Dead tired, we rested and ate a meager meal of rice and fish, and then, in pouring rain, trudged back through the dreary landscape.

Could the largest flower in the world be going the way of the dodo bird and the passenger pigeon, even before its life history became known? No botanist had ever written that *Rafflesia arnoldi* was endangered, let alone threatened with extinction. Plants are often not rare, just hard to find.

Weary and disappointed as I was, I simply refused to believe that *Rafflesia* no longer existed. Passing villages and fields while discussing other areas where the plant might be, we were cheered up by friendly greetings from rice farmers and children. There was one more known area where I might see and photograph the flower. This last known habitat was outside the small village of Bukit Tinggi, where we arrived a few days later.

The first sight was disheartening. Next to the sign declaring the area to be a reserve, a giant tree supporting a host vine needed by *Rafflesia* had just been felled and lay across the path. Its top branches touched the newly dug, encroaching rice paddies. I wondered what Sir Stamford Raffles would have said if he had seen the endless rice paddies where once had been the lush rain forest he so greatly admired.

After searching the entire area until late afternoon we at last came across one magnificent specimen, half hidden among the thick vines hanging down from the canopy. The huge mottled brown flower sprang from a wrist-thick stem of a giant climbing liana, *Cissus augustifolia*. *Rafflesia* is a true parasitic plant without green parts, leaves, a stem, and roots. Evolution has stripped *Rafflesia* of irrelevant organs, which have atrophied into functionless forms. Unable to manufacture food for itself, it lives at the expense of its host and is totally dependent on the sap produced by the liana for nourishment. The liana must produce enough sap for itself as well as for its gigantic parasite.

An odd plant, *Rafflesia* was once thought to be a fungus, but it is now known to be a member of the seed-bearing plants. It is inconspicuous until the bud appears on the host liana. The bud, which resembles a cabbage, takes many months to develop, when it opens with a hissing sound. The fact that the bud takes so long to mature and is located where the liana touches the ground makes the plant vulnerable to destruction by careless tourists drawn by radio announcements and newspaper articles describing where the plant had been seen flowering.

Rafflesia arnoldi is only one striking example of the unimaginable surprises and interesting relationships one can find in the rain forest.

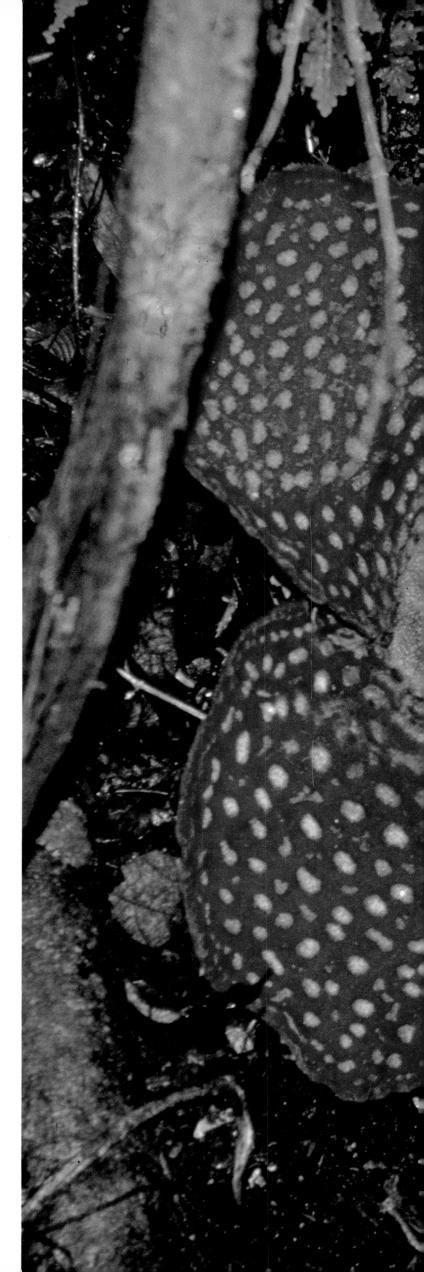

This time my goal was to find and explore a virgin rain forest. In Manaus, Brazil, I rented an open boat and hired Carlos, a guide who had aided me on previous occasions, and some helpers. For three days we journeyed up the Amazon River, often in the company of porpoises, until we reached and followed a tributary, and then a smaller tributary. When we finally went ashore to make our first camp, we saw the kind of rain forest described in countless adventure stories: a seemingly solid wall of creeping vines wove the trees of the riverbank into a near-impenetrable green fortress and gave the canopy an appearance of phenomenal density. The old pathway into the rain forest was so overgrown with creeping vines and bushy vegetation that to get in we had to use our machetes.

Except for a few small forest palms with finely pleated fronds, some showy caladiums, and the ever-present saplings with elegant, glossy, drip-tip leaves, the glistening humid ground was quite barren. The impoverished laterite clay in this disturbed forest was so hard that I could barely dig into it with my machete.

In the afternoon we decided to make camp. Wielding his machete with the effortless strokes of a master, Carlos brought down a fourteen-foot-long sapling. With long thin pieces of bark stripped and split from another tree, he tied the sapling among three trees above our hammocks, making an ideal support for the canvas that would protect us from rain. He also made a table to keep my camera equipment dry and above ground. That evening, lying there in the hammock, I listened to the soft, steady rain. The next morning it would evaporate into a steamy mist and then come down again as early afternoon showers, thus continually recycling.

We left camp the following morning at six o'clock under partly cloudy skies. After an eight-hour hike we came to a stream where gigantic boulders had made it next to impossible for loggers to transport any of the huge trees on the other side out of the forest. Yearly flooding and sunlight available at all levels at the edge of the stream had created exuberant growth conditions, enabling fast-growing saplings and vines to spring up as a dense undergrowth. But past the boulder area, as Carlos had promised, was a virgin rain forest, delightfully undisturbed.

What a contrast! The change from the blinding sunshine to the twilight-dark interior of the rain forest was startling. I could hardly see anything. As my eyes became accustomed to the interior, I saw isolated specks of sunlight filtering through the dense foliage, dancing down to the bare ground and leaving a faint diffused greenish light to give a shadowless substance to the dim forest interior.

I took out my light meter; it read six stops between the brilliant light outside and the dim light on the forest floor, an incredible difference which meant that only about 2 percent of the light reached the forest floor.

The temperature had plummeted from an oppressive 90°F near the riverbank to a comfortable 70°F. The smell in the still air was heavy and earthy but not pungent. In the distance howler monkeys made a sound reminiscent of the eerie, lonely call of wolves. Then the deep quiet returned.

There was surprisingly little underbrush. As if by a magic hand, it seemed that all the luxuriant vegetation had been cast from the forest floor onto the tree branches and trunks and left hanging there. Epiphytic orchids, bromeliads, mosses, and ferns were heaped on trunks and branches among the crustose design of lichens.

Stately trees rose to a height of 160 feet and formed a canopy 100 feet across. The flattened buttressed roots reached up 25 feet to make veritable walls at the bases of tall trees. Arm-thick lianas festooned with green moss and epiphytes were gracefully looped from tree to tree, from canopy to canopy, weaving them together into a lofty roof. It was as if nature had made its own hushed, dim cathedral. I could not help but marvel at the lianas stretching down from the canopy, taut as violin strings, anchoring in the ground. I slapped one with my open hand. Two seconds later the oscillations in the liana returned like an echo.

We walked along what seemed like a natural path and suddenly found ourselves blocked by a giant fallen tree that had torn out several young trees when it had crashed to the ground, exposing a surprisingly shallow one-foot-deep root system. In the rain forest the enormous trunk of a fallen tree quickly becomes riddled by termites. The invisible clearinghouse of fungi and bacteria sap and break down the wood for sun-loving saplings, which in competition smother each other in their struggle to reach the canopy.

Passing by a clearing which must have been used by Indians years ago, we discovered some overgrown cacao trees (*Theobroma cacao,* meaning "drink of the gods"). These had clusters of small white flowers growing directly on the trunks. Some of the clusters had developed into ten-inch, football-shaped pods which contained the seeds from which chocolate is made. Some of the pods were yellow and ripe. The pulp around the seeds is highly aromatic and tasty and gave us all a most delicious cool refreshment.

In a clearing near a stream I noticed a magnificent yellow-billed toucan feeding in a tree. As I was about to mount my gunsight-telephoto lens, my helper called "*Beija-flor*" (flower-kisser:hummingbird). I ran over to where the iridescent green-blue hummingbird was feeding— on a large flower of the cannonball tree. I quickly put the macrozoom lens on the camera and told my helper to hold the electronic flash. Just as everything was right to take the pictures, the bird flew away. Nevertheless, I saw that other insect pollinators were interested in the curving, sculptured white-and-magenta flower: a magnificently colored riodinid butterfly hovered near the flower, and a trail of ants conveniently made use of the smooth roots of an epiphytic *Philodendron* climber to reach their prize. I took my semiautomatic diaphragm device, which I had constructed from a microscope lens for extreme close-up photography. Just as I was ready to photograph the butterfly and marching ants, a cannonballfruit came crashing to the ground, whizzing by my left shoulder. When I weighed the iron-hard fruit (two pounds), I counted myself lucky to have missed a good headache and changed my mind about photographing the butterfly and ants.

Following the widening stream, I managed to photograph my first basilisk—or, as natives call it, Jesu Cristo lizard—which when frightened runs quickly over the surface of the water on its two webbed hind feet. When it slows down, it sinks and begins to swim.

Next to the stream, tree trunks provided the specialized habitat needed for some climbers. A *Peperomia* vine was growing in its characteristic flattened symmetrical zigzag pattern for fifteen feet up the trunk. Tree branches supported copious plant growth: I climbed up a tree to photograph the most exotic of these epiphytes, such as orchids and bromeliads. Next to my perch I counted twelve different species! A *Cattleya* orchid was fully six inches across. Viable seed from this orchid alone can number half a million, contributing to a constant "rain" of seeds in the rain forest. Only a few seeds find the right habitat for survival for an orchid, on only one or a few kinds of trees, only on the shady or sunny side of the trunk, etc.

Next to me on the branch was a rosette-shaped bromeliad, the leaves overlapped tightly like the wrapper of a fat cigar, forming a leak-proof bowl of water. Here I photographed mosquito larvae wiggling on the surface, a spider lurking in ambush, a hurrying ant, and a feeding beetle. As a bonus I got a picture of four small bromeliad flowers just above the surface of the water inside the bowl. A smaller bromeliad of the genus *Tillandsia* had narrow pointed red leaves around the flower stalk, which grew in a cluster at the fork of the branch.

Sitting on the branch I realized that one misses much of the plant and animal life when walking through a tropical rain forest. Aloft on a branch in the sunlit canopy it is far easier to hear, see, and identify birds, flowers and their pollinators, brilliant butterflies, lizards, reptiles, and small mammals. In this respect the tropical rain forest can be compared with tropical oceans: both have distinct, vertical life-gradients, which increase in species with increasing sunlight. In both environments the most highly colored species are found in the highest level, where the sun is strongest. As the intensity of the sunlight diminishes, so do the colors of the species.

The challenge of trying to spot concealed animals or unusual plants in this dripping tropical rain forest is a constant delight. I found that the best way to photograph specimens was to have one helper about twenty to thirty feet on my right, another at the same distance on my left, and one behind holding my strobes. We all advanced together, looking for concealed specimens on the bark of the trunks, on epiphytic growth, under leaves, etc., and each having a share of discovering things to photograph.

We devised a way to test our abilities to spot insects and reptiles on tree trunks. First we counted what we could spot; then, brushing gently up and down the sides of the trunk with a twiggy branch, we would watch for specimens to jump or fly away. One of my helpers consistently found nearly twice as many specimens as I did.

Once, I found myself staring at an interesting knot formation on the smooth mottled bark of a giant buttressed tree, when suddenly the knot stretched out a leg, shattering the illusion. Only because it moved did I spot this mottled tree frog, just a few inches away.

Patient observation was vital and always rewarding. We examined every bit of bark, shrub, leaf at a snail's pace, as if they contained priceless treasures. I was reminded of the scientist Louis Agassiz, who found great drama in everyday things around him: "I spent the summer traveling. I got half-way across my back yard."

In no forms of life are the survival strategies of species more graphically visible than in the mimicry, concealment, bluff, and warning games of the moths found in the rain forests. The thousands of moths I have observed and photographed in rain forests around the world have an amazing ability to invade a variety of biological niches and to exploit all possible—and even some seemingly impossible—ecological microhabitats. One of the most common and undoubtedly successful places of concealment for moths is among bark, lichen, and fungi. Noctuid and geometrid moths and moths of many other families reinforce the effect of their mottled green cloaks and tufted forelegs (which often look like the filaments of spreading lichen) by aligning themselves with the cracks of the bark.

On the jungle path in New Guinea I often found moths that looked like twigs on trunks or twigs that had fallen from the canopy and had landed on lower leaves. On looking closely at such a "twig," I was surprised to discover that it was a geometrid caterpillar, frozen into position. Entranced by this particularly clever mimic, I arranged my lights and carelessly reached toward another small stick that I wanted to remove from the picture. Suddenly the "stick" crept a few inches away and carefully repositioned itself. A close look revealed it to be a tiny notodontid moth. No wonder it takes the sharp eyes of a bird to detect this perfect camouflage.

Even plants protect themselves against predators, and one of their important defense mechanisms is to become saturated by poisonous compounds. However, many insects turn this to their advantage by eating and storing the compounds, and eventually becoming distasteful to the palates of predators such as birds and lizards. Experiments have shown that birds and lizards are very adept at learning to avoid these insects: after having tasted its first bitter insect, a bird will hesitate the next time. A second or third try is often enough to implant the lesson for life.

To advertise to predators that they are distasteful, some insects exhibit hues in gaudy combinations of yellow, orange, red, black, and blue. To the moth, evolution bestowed talents of make-believe, bluffing, and a seemingly endless variety of strategies for survival. Of course, moths do not mimic just mere green leaves, but mimic leaves in every imaginable state: buds of leaves; skeletonized leaves;

curled-up leaves; fallen leaves; swaying leaves, etc.

A moth I photographed in Malaya looked exactly like half of a dead, dried leaf, complete with crumpled outline and leaf-miner markings, and with its legs the moth even imitated remnant veins of the already deteriorated portion of the leaf!

I seldom have a chance actually to see a bird or a lizard call the bluff and pick out a concealed moth. Once, however, I saw a bird near Sarawak watching a tasty-looking little morsel on top of a slightly swaying green leaf. The bird decided to go after it and swooped down and snapped up the little thing—and to my surprise immediately spat it out and flew away. Eagerly I went over and picked it up. It was just a little shriveled-up brown leaf!

Leeches are everywhere in the tropical rain forest, especially in the wet grass on the forest floor in slightly disturbed areas. I found them especially numerous near logging camps in Sri Lanka. Although we all were careful about tucking the ends of our pants inside our socks, the leeches still found their way through the tiniest opening and our shoes soon became sloshing red with blood. Leeches move rather rapidly in a looping manner like that of inch or measuring worms. Two of them managed to crawl inside my shirt and had fastened themselves to my back. Leeches immediately inject an anticoagulant and a painkilling compound, so that the host is not even aware that they are there. Riding back to the lodge in the jeep late that afternoon, I leaned comfortably back and, without knowing it, burst two small, fat blood sausages so the entire back of my shirt turned a vivid red, greatly alarming our hostess when we arrived that evening. When photographing or exploring the rain forest one must be prepared to sacrifice some blood.

Arriving at the orangutan rain-forest reserve near Sandakan, Sabah, I was delighted to find the animals easily observable. Having grown up in Drøbak, on the Oslo fjord in Norway, with only a television knowledge of what the creatures are like, I could hardly believe my eyes when I saw them. They swung at the end of long lianas, back and forth, back and forth, kicking away from large tree trunks for renewed momentum. When climbing a young supple tree, they seemed to know how far down toward the ground they could bend it before it snapped. Their bodies seemed all hair and muscles with four look-alike arms and legs.

Observing and photographing orangutans for days on end, I was impressed to see the subtle but persistent process by which they learned to differentiate edible plants from poisonous or distasteful ones. They simply broke off a small piece of vegetation and let it dangle from their lips to taste it for a while before they dropped it and picked out another piece to be tasted. One young orangutan made my day by coming up to me, putting its warm hand in mine, and walking with me for a while on the forest path.

Tropical rain forests with their lush vegetation are natural laboratories where we find spectacular examples of the intricacies of evolution and natural selection. In the Amazonian forest, with its proliferation of species, one could spend an entire lifetime attempting to learn the interrelationships and behavior of the animals inhabiting a single square mile—and still leave a wealth of fascinating material unexplored.

Man's excessive deforestation and slash-and-burn agricultural methods have altered the original predator-prey relationships developed during millions of years. In many areas the balance has been irretrievably lost and the natural habitat to a large extent no longer exists, accelerating the rate at which species are becoming extinct. Thus, many small animals are forced out of existence before we know anything of their behavior and interesting life histories.

The remaining uncut virgin tropical rain forests of the world are located in relatively small areas, which are now exceedingly vulnerable to human influence, such as in Costa Rica, Puerto Rico, Nepal, Sikkim, Sabah, Madagascar, Malay, the Philippines, and Queensland, Australia. In Central America one-third of the forests have already disappeared, and worldwide, forests are disappearing at a rate of fifty acres per minute, day and night, at a pace as fast as men and machines can do it. In a short time—surely within the life span of most people alive today—most rain forests will no longer exist if help does not come soon.

Nearly all our staple food today—corn, wheat, rice, fruits, potatoes—are highly developed horticultural varieties. We need from time to time to draw on the genetic material from their original wild strains in nature for new improvements and protection from viral diseases. When we destroy natural environments, we destroy this genetic material that we may someday need.

Many people are voicing deep concern about the future of the rain forests, warning that their destruction would be a calamity. S. Dillon Ripley, Secretary of the Smithsonian Institution, says "...we cannot afford to continue altering nature, in blind ignorance, without risking irreversible changes that could threaten our own survival." But it seems that a positive reaction has set in around the world. Nations are beginning to legislate the protection of endangered plants and animals. During my recent visits to many forest reserves and national parks, I observed that as people learn more about their natural environment they take pride in their own unique forests as a natural heritage and become more concerned about saving them. For example, Costa Rica and Sabah are not only protecting but enlarging existing parks and reserves. If this trend continues and still more legislation is enacted, there certainly is hope for *Rafflesia* in the future.

Kjell B. Sandved
National Museum of Natural History
Smithsonian Institution, Washington, D.C.

Introduction: My First Encounter

I have to confess that it was really the tales of voluptuous women, magnetic steel bands, and inexpensive rum that made the newly advertised position in Trinidad so irresistibly attractive. The source of my information was the flow of young agricultural officers who arrived in Nigeria after a year of training in Trinidad at the Imperial College of Tropical Agriculture. Union Jack in hand, these idealistic men and women were committed to change the world. However, they soon discovered that they were woefully ill-prepared for aspects of their work that were not itemized in the job description. They were, for example, unskilled in the martial art of amputating the appendages of persons trapped under overturned "mammywagons," as the open trucks are known, which careened along the dirt roads overloaded with human cargo. The drivers of these megahearses usually escaped disaster by leaping out at the last possible moment and vanishing into the bush. One wonders, in retrospect, if that was the real reason why the cabs always lacked doors.

Prior to arriving in Trinidad, my own experiences in the tropics had been confined to the semiarid regions of northern Nigeria, where there were four or five rainless months each year between January and June. At the end of the dry season, the pounding rain on the corrugated iron roofs would raise our ecstasy to levels so high that we would run outside and gambol in the downpour, fully clothed. We knew then that the dust of the Harmattan was laid to rest for another year, the cavernous cracks in the furniture would heal, and the foliage would green-up and flourish once again.

I had been at my new job at the Imperial College of Tropical Agriculture, affectionately known as "ICTA," for only a few days when the Principal invited his new zoologist to join him on a trip to the rain forest. He was going to collect some tree-fern trunks which, when cut up into short lengths, make ideal rooting material for aerial orchids. We drove along a narrow road paved only with two parallel strips of lumpy blacktop, recently dug out of the pitch lake at La Brea and pounded into the ground. Roads metaled with strips of tarmacadam are not uncommon in the tropics, for there is a saving in both labor and materials. Even the most outwardly docile tropical driver engages daily in the game of "chicken" when meeting oncoming traffic, for he leaves the relative comfort and safety of the strips only at the last possible moment. However, the most persistent annoyance is that the strips always seem to have been designed to fit an axle width which is quite different from that of the vehicle being driven.

From the road, the forest seemed impenetrable; it arose on the right as a sheer wall of solid green reaching well over a hundred feet. On the left, without retaining walls or natural barriers of any kind, was a precipitous drop several times that distance. My principal concern was less over the quality of the road surface than with the direction in which we were pointing, for my nonchalant driver, in addition to being an orchid fancier, was an ardent ornithologist and spared no effort to ensure that I missed none of the avian splendors that were passing by at a very rapid rate.

At last we reached our goal. The only way into the forest was along a stream bed, for without a machete the penetration of the forest face would have been impossible. However, once inside, the light was mellow, the temperature was cool, and walking was relatively easy. The forest floor was carpeted with fallen branches and a scanty layer of leaves, threadbare in places where naked earth showed through. Herbs were conspicuously rare. The massive trunks of the larger trees were widely separated and arose straight out of the ground without branching for fifty or sixty feet (15–18 m). Between the trees were saplings, tree ferns, palms, and a few low shrubs, but there was still sufficient room to walk without stooping, except to protect one's eyes. Care had to be taken not to trip over an exposed root or fallen log.

We climbed a bank and found a tree fern with a trunk about eight inches (20 cm) in "diameter at breast height" (abbreviated by foresters to dbh). With a handsaw we felled it near the base, topped the fallen trunk, and rolled it down the slope. It was at this point that I realized why I had been invited to take part in the excursion. My companion had a bad back! I had just straddled the log and was preparing to lift when I heard quietly, but firmly, "Don't move. Stay exactly where you are. I'll go and fetch my gun." It was not only because he was the Principal that I obeyed, but because not more than ten inches from my leg and hand was a large bushmaster (*Lachesis muta*), a lethally venomous snake. I was rooted, hardly even daring to move my eyeballs. The delay seemed interminable, but at last the gunner returned and dispatched the snake, and almost my foot, with a single blast. The bisected corpse later graced the departmental museum with a suitable label prominently displayed.

Nine years in Trinidad was a memorable experience, enhanced by intimate contact with the William Beebe Tropical Research Station, which was latterly supported by both the New York Zoological Society and Rockefeller University. The facility was a haven for tropical biologists, for it stood on a promontory entirely surrounded by rain forest. The house itself used to be the country seat of the governor of Trinidad and Tobago, where, far from the madding crowds of Port of Spain, he and his family could enjoy seclusion and peace. In 1949, Dr. William Beebe, tropical natural historian and traveler of bathysphere fame, purchased the property and gave it to his lifelong employer, the New York Zoological Society. The new field station of the Department of Tropical Research was christened "Simla" in reminiscence of his travels and of that town in India.

With failing health and advancing years, Will Beebe escaped the New York winters by spending more and more time in Trinidad; in 1962 at the age of 85 he died at his beloved Simla and was laid to rest in the tropical setting to which he had devoted his life. Beebe was one of the last of a rare breed of biologists: a master of quiet observation who not only thought intelligently but one who had, in the words of William Henry Davies, "time to stand and stare."

The house itself became a biologists' mecca and attracted

researchers from Japan, Germany, England, Canada, the United States, and many other parts of the world. They came to study birds, bats, snakes, lizards, frogs, insects, and, all too rarely, plants. Simla was the realization of Will Beebe's dreams, a place where scientists could become engrossed in their work without interference or distraction. During one summer, while northern universities were without formal classes, we were visited by Nbuo Suga, Stewart Swihart, and Hubert Markl studying the nervous systems of katydids, butterflies, and ants; Dorothy Dunning, Roderick Suthers, Donald Griffin, and some of his graduate students working on the behavior of bats; John Turner and the late Philip Sheppard investigating butterfly genetics; Lincoln Brower and his very able undergraduate students from Amherst College unraveling the mysteries of mimicry; as well as Peter Scott and Jan Lindblad, who were making scientific films for English and Swedish television. Living and working alongside such a diversity of erudite biologists was a unique opportunity. The mealtime conversations and discussions over methods and materials assured that we all grew professionally in each other's company.

For the liberal-minded visitor, Trinidad was not just a research experience but a close encounter with a new kind of life, for the *joie de vivre* of the Trinidadians and their hedonistic commitment to pleasure and enjoyment was a model for all to envy. The pulsating music of the steel bands and the flamboyant rhythms of the dancers produced moments of delight that would be hard to equal anywhere in the world. Add to that the travel-poster beaches with warm, shark-free water, and the only missing ingredient from this tropical utopia was good underwater visibility. The scuba diver or snorkeler has to travel twenty-one miles to Tobago for the completion of a vacation paradise.

Because Trinidad has been separated from the mainland of South America for less than seventeen thousand years, this politically independent country is ideal for tropical research. The fauna and flora are typical of the nearby continent, while the island has an international airport, good roads, and an English-speaking population. The biology of the island has been well-studied by visitors and the faculty and students of the University of the West Indies at St. Augustine. J. S. Beard's work on the forest vegetation is prominent among the scanty publications that have appeared on tropical rain forests between the English translation of Andreas Schimper's monumental German tome in 1903 and Paul Richards's classic *The Tropical Rain Forest,* which was published in 1952.

Academic research in the United States reached its peak during the mid- to late 1960s, for, with the impetus of Sputnik still running strong, the National Science Foundation and other granting agencies were well-funded and evangelical in their promotion of a wide spectrum of projects. Since those balmy days, we have seen a steady decline in the support for tropical research and, more particularly, a hostility from certain quarters toward projects whose direct relevance to human needs is not immediately

Opposite. (top) *Popularized by the advertisements for Guinness in Europe, the toucan is a figure of fun. No animal should look so ridiculous. The colors on the bill are species recognition signals and a painted-out male would be doomed to a life of perpetual celibacy. This is the keel-billed toucan* (Ramphastos sulphureus) *from Central America.*

(center) *The Southeast Asian orchid group to which* Cirrhopetalum rothschildianum *belongs has ingenious devices for temporarily capturing flies and forcing them to act as pollinators. Seeking the source of an attractive odor, a fly walks on its hinged petals and is flicked against a pad of entangling hooks. The struggling fly eventually escapes through a hazard-free corridor, but not before it has been burdened with a package of pollen to be deposited on the next flower it visits.*

(bottom) *Stink bugs* (Pentatomidae) *are so-called with good reason. When handled, insects such as this* Arocera spectabilis *from Amazonas, Brazil, exude a vile-smelling fluid from a pair of glands on the thorax. Judging by the conspicuous color pattern, the protection afforded by the chemical makes it profitable to advertise the potential discomfort a predator would experience.*

Left. (top) *The web of an orb weaver from Sri Lanka makes a beautiful subject for early morning photography.*

(bottom) *Orchids come in a spectacular array of shapes, colors, and sizes. This one is* Cirrhopetalum amesianum, *found in Malaya.*

obvious. To stand a good chance of being funded today, a botanist's research project should be directed toward the discovery of a new source of fuel, drug, or food. Relatively little enthusiasm can be expected for a study of basic plant biology. These changes in attitudes by the administrators of funding agencies, public figures, and Congress correctly reflect the indifference of the average citizen and have inevitably weakened the viability of tropical field stations. Although it is sad that William Beebe did not live to see Simla reach its academic zenith, it would have been cruel for him to witness its demise in 1971, for it then lost its financial support and its association with American researchers. Since 1974 it has served only as overflow accommodation for the nearby Asa Wright Nature Center.

It is tragic that, because of inadequate funding or political instability, the tropical research stations of the world are in such acute jeopardy. Research stations in many tropical countries have become dominated by politics, or have been given over exclusively to applied research in agriculture or medicine. The rain forests are in dire need of thorough understanding, yet there are few places left where scientists can work without fear of arrest or of being held for ransom. Most critically, we are running out of time. It has been estimated that at currently increasing rates of destruction, virtually all rain forests of the tropical world will have been felled by the end of this century. The forests will be gone before we have had time to understand them.

Viewed from Afar

Modern-life expectations continually goad us to hasten the fulfillment of our destinies and leave us little time to contemplate the past. Inevitably, the present is a product of the past and a balanced view of current events requires an appreciation of history. The short span of a schoolchild's life makes his or her understanding of retrospection unlikely, but for the mature adult who has gained a sense of time, the study of origins and roots offers an unrivaled insight into the nature of contemporary problems.

Any analysis of a situation benefits inordinately from a sense of perspective. If we resist the temptation to grapple immediately with detail and instead stand back and view the rain forests from afar, we will be able to understand their paradoxical complexity. The rain forests are real: we can smell them, see them, taste them, feel them, even measure them. But they are not static, just awaiting our attention; instead, they are dynamic systems which we witness at one brief point in time. Rain forests have had a long and tortuous history. They have undergone massive changes during the last hundred million years and will change as much again during the years to come. The awesome question we must ultimately ask ourselves is how human activity, as an instrument of environmental change, is affecting the natural order and what effect these changes will have on the future of the rain forests. But first we must return to basics, examine the chronicle of the rain forests, and acquire a sense of historical perspective.

During the first half of this century, biological geographers tied themselves in mental knots trying to explain the puzzling distributions of both ancient and modern animals and plants. They have had cause to blush, for now that we understand the motions of the continents, their explanations seem puerile. The changing shapes of the land, together with dramatic changes in the global climate, have had a profound effect on both the fauna and flora. Paleontologists, for example, were frustrated by the fossilized presence of the reptile *Mesosaurus* in 250-million-year-old rocks in eastern South America and western South Africa. How could such a small animal cross such a wide and treacherous sea passage? And if it could, why did it not also occur elsewhere?

The answer now seems simple. At the time those reptiles were alive, the continents were united and enjoying a tropical climate. Astronauts visiting us 200 million years ago, perhaps in one of Erich von Daniken's celestial chariots (*Chariots of the Gods?*), would have found the earth a very different place from the one we know today. The most obvious difference would probably have been that all the land was coalesced into a single mass. About 150 million years ago, the supercontinent Pangea began to break up, initially into the northern Laurasia and southern Gondwanaland separated by the Tethys Sea, and latterly into the pieces we presently recognize as continents. Every schoolchild has noticed, as did Francis Bacon in 1620, that the coastlines of the Atlantic seaboards have a generally similar shape, but if one compares the edge of the continental shelf, rather than the wave-eroded beach lines recorded on an atlas, the goodness-of-fit is astonishingly accurate.

Although Antonio Snider Pellegrini hinted at the idea of drifting continents in 1858, it was not until the publications of the German astronomer-meteorologist Alfred Wegener between 1912 and 1924 that a recognized scientist attached his reputation to such a radical proposition. Wegener was regarded as a heretic by all except the American Frederick B. Taylor, and his theories continued to be ridiculed for nearly half a century. I well remember my own geology professor in 1950, at the Royal College of Science in London, dismissing Wegener's ideas on continental drift in less than a minute as those of an ignorant crank.

Wegener's evidence rested largely upon the similarity of the outlines of the eastern and western Atlantic coasts, and the presence of unusual rock formations at correlated positions on either side of the ocean. The most serious objection that Wegener himself could not overcome, and which is still controversial, was "How?" How could continents, made of rock, drift? But the adage "as hard as a rock" is misleading. A stick of sealing wax will snap if it is bent suddenly—it behaves like a rock, but if left projecting over the edge of a bench for a week, it will be found to have curved down in response to the weak but continuous force of gravity. The comparison is apt, for the coarse-grained granite and fine basalt that compose the inner layers of the earth's crust are hard and brittle, but when subjected to continuous pressure from within the earth, they behave as a highly viscous fluid and flow in the same manner as ice at the bottom of a glacier. We still do not know the nature of the physical forces that cause the continents to drift, but one presumes that they are convection currents arising within the deeper and hotter portions of the earth.

Today, Alfred Wegener's theory of continental drift is widely accepted, but even its acceptance invites a new set of questions for the biogeographer. When and in what sequence did Pangea break up? How long did each fragment spend in temperate, tropical, or subtropical climates? The answers to such questions have a direct bearing on the history of the rain forests of each region. We would then know the opportunities the organisms had for movement between adjacent continents, the duration of periods of isolation, and the adaptations that would have been necessary to endure the rigors of the climate.

Within the present general pattern of climatic latitudinal belts, local variations have profound effects on the vegetation. Of particular interest are the warm offshore, water-laden winds that are driven upward by the Rocky Mountains in the states of Oregon and Washington. The cooled air deposits its burden of moisture on the Pacific slopes and supports the most extensive rain forests known at temperate latitudes. These unique and impressive coniferous rain forests are protected from disturbance in the Olympic National Park in northwestern Washington State.

Turning our attention to the tropical rain forest, we find that 90 percent of the present forest flora is composed of

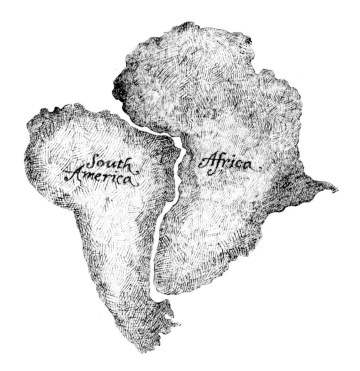

flowering plants. Fossil studies suggest that these kinds of plants have existed for less than 150 million years. This historical situation means that at the time Pangea broke up, there were no flowering plants comparable to modern forms. The microscopical examination of ultrathin sections of rock in which plant remains are fossilized shows us that the rich tropical forests were composed of nonflowering conifers, ginkgoes, cycads, horsetails, ferns, and many other treelike plants that are now either extinct or reduced to relatively minor components of the tropical flora.

One of the more popular views among modern botanists is that the flowering plants developed in the drier areas to the north of the tropical belt, for the tropics were already flourishing with forest plants. The flowering plants, developing in concert with the aerial insects, were so successful that during extended periods of more arid climates they invaded the tropical regions and became established as the dominant type of vegetation.

Pollen analysis of sediments deposited on the Atlantic sea floor over the last few hundred thousand years has shown that during glacial periods the flora of tropical West Africa was characteristic of not only a cooler climate but one that was much drier than is known today. Thus, during the ice ages, the southward shift and increased aridity of the climatic belts were manifest in the vegetation, and the tropical rain forest was squeezed almost out of existence in America and Africa. Data from fossils and the contemporary distribution of both animals and plants indicate that instead of forming a continuous equatorial belt, the rain forests of these continents were fragmented into relic islands, each widely separated by grasslands or even deserts. Until recently, the tropical rain forest was considered a permanently stable community of great antiquity, but researchers on Amazonia have exposed a mosaic pattern of organisms with an apparently homogeneous habitat. It seems unlikely that such geographical diversity has great durability, and implies that the rain forest is undergoing constant change.

It is the geological and climatic history that holds the clues to the history of the rain forests. Thirty thousand years ago, and perhaps even more recently, the rain forests of Amazonia and probably at least the eastern parts of central Africa were reduced to a patchwork of hardy survivors, resisting the vicissitudes of an increasingly hostile arid climate. Within these forest islands, breeding isolation and local adaptation allowed differentiation of forms which, when reunited with their neighbors, found interbreeding blocked by physical or behavioral difficulties. The newly formed species now live side by side and account, in part, for the extraordinary diversity seen in forest habitats.

Today, the tropical rain forests are made up of some species that have a long tropical history and some others that have been derived relatively recently from temperate ancestors. Distinguishing which plants of the tropical rain forest are recent arrivals and which have a distant tropical heritage is a problem with which tropical botanists are only just beginning to grapple.

Left. *Although the rain forest itself is uniform, the topography can be most varied. This view of an ancient water course in Bukit Tinggi, Sumatra, shows the steep escarpments. The forest in situations such as this has "edges," where lianas, herbs, shrubs, and epiphytes abound. Bukit Tinggi lies almost exactly on the equator.*

Above. *There are few experiences to match looking out over the forest canopy after a rainstorm and breathing in the gloriously fresh air, slightly perfumed with the fragrance of moist vegetation. This scene is at Tovar, on the slopes of the Andes in Venezuela.*

Opposite (top) *This cloud forest at Horton Plains, Sri Lanka, is under pressure from grazing livestock, so the interface of the forest and the grassland is unnaturally sharp. Such a sudden discontinuity overemphasizes the density of the cloud forest but does show the small stature of the trees and the relatively few canopy layers.*

(bottom) *At seven thousand feet (2,120 m), this open area of the canopy in the forest at Cibodja in Java is maintained by an 176°F (80°C) spring in which blue-green algae flourish.*

Above. *The modern tropical biologist still must be an adventurer. Walking over this suspension bridge in Wau, New Guinea, takes more courage than skill as it undulates and sways high over the silt-laden river.*

Following pages. *Watching the sun rise over the mountains of Ratnapura in Sri Lanka would make a splendid start to the day if human beings had not almost totally denuded the hills of their natural forest vegetation.*

A Coarse-grained Picture

Most of the rain forests of the world occur on the major land masses in a belt with its own midline centered 5 degrees north of the geographical equator. The rain forests extend beyond the Tropic of Capricorn only in Argentina and eastern Australia, and northward above the Tropic of Cancer only in Burma. Within these regions, the rain forests are interrupted by unfavorable local conditions. Deserts and grasslands dominate where low rainfall, low temperatures, or high winds inhibit the growth of trees; swamps appear where semipermanent waterlogging of the soil allows only the growth of specialized vegetation, such as palms; and volcanic soils may be too young to have developed a clothing of rain forest.

The most dense stands of tropical rain forest occur in Central America from eastern Mexico to northern Colombia and western Ecuador; southeast Cuba and Puerto Rico; the Amazon and Orinoco basins; equatorial western and west-central Africa; eastern Madagascar; western peninsular India and Sri Lanka; peripheral Burma, eastern Vietnam, western Thailand, and the Malay peninsula; the islands of Indonesia; the Philippines; and eastern Australia. Although occupying similar climatic zones with an annual precipitation of more than sixty inches (1,600 mm) which is fairly evenly distributed throughout the year, with an annual temperature of 68° to 82°F (20°–28°C), the individual history of each continent has keenly affected both the appearance and distribution of each rain forest.

About eighty-five million years ago the continent of South America lost contact with Africa and became an island drifting slowly northwest. All the animals on the land mass at that time adapted to the changing conditions independently of those in the rest of the world and thus acquired characteristics that were quite unique. About twenty-five million years ago, by which time South America had assumed approximately its present position, the western edge of the continent began to be subjected to the severe buckling which ultimately gave rise to the Andean mountain chain and which had a dramatic effect on the geography of the continent. Prior to this collision of the South American plate with the Nazca plate under the Pacific Ocean, the main drainage of the continent flowed from the very old rocks of the uplifted Brazilian Shield into an inland sea which opened to the northwest, where Colombia is now. With the continued uplift of the Andes, the northwestern sea drained and was reclaimed by the land, first as a salt marsh as the sea was cut off and then as freshwater marsh and latterly as dry land. The rise of the Andes caused the drainage to change from east to west, to west to east, and the Amazon River was born.

About the same time, the continent of North America suffered buckling where the western edge of the North American plate met the edge of the immovable Pacific plate. The mountain building continued and in Central America became manifest initially as a chain of islands in the ocean between southern California and central Colombia. It was not until about five million years ago that these islands coalesced as the isthmus of Central America, and the continuous land connection between North and South America was complete.

Once the continuity of the Central American isthmus was established, even the most sedentary organisms with weak dispersal potential had the opportunity of extending their range. Some of the more mobile animals and plants had already used the precursor islands as stepping stones and had increased their distribution north or south.

Many southern animals and plants became established in Central America but relatively few settled in the northern continent, the hummingbird, perhaps, being one of the most conspicuous exceptions. It is only during recent times that the South and Central American armadillo and opossum have become successful in the United States and are annually enlarging their range.

In contrast, more North American animals, including deer, tapirs, and the camel-like llamas, entered South America and survived there. Ironically, the northern cousins of the tapir and llamas became extinct in North America and so these animals are now considered typically South American.

As the animals and plants of Central and South America are essentially similar, biogeographers have applied the word Neotropica to the combination of the two regions. It is in northern Mexico that the southern elements of the fauna and flora give way to those of North America, or Nearctica as it is more properly known.

With the beginning of the last retreat of the glaciers, about seventeen thousand years ago, the vegetative zones of the world began to return to their present positions. One must always remember that the melting of the polar caps released enough water to raise the level of the oceans by about 360 feet (110 m). The effect of this rise in sea level has been to inundate portions of the continental shelf and partition off portions of the mainland as "continental" islands. Trinidad is such an island; broadly connected to mainland South America, it was cut off by rising waters only during the last fifteen thousand years. The fauna and flora are thus essentially similar to that of neighboring Venezuela, but with the loss of some species that have not been able to withstand the hazards of island life.

Due to the influence of temperate climates, the rain forest at its northern limits in Mexico, Cuba, and Puerto Rico lacks the extremes of diversity, stature, and luxuriance seen in the equatorial forests of Amazonia. Traveling south through the relics of the rain forest in the highly populated areas of Central America, the characteristic features become more obvious until the full richness is found across the watershed of the Amazon in southeastern Colombia.

Within the Amazon basin, two categories of land can be distinguished: the terra firma, which is not flooded, and the várzea, or floodplains. The rain forest discussed here is typically found on the terra firma, for the várzea is colonized only by plants that can withstand three to four months of continuous inundation.

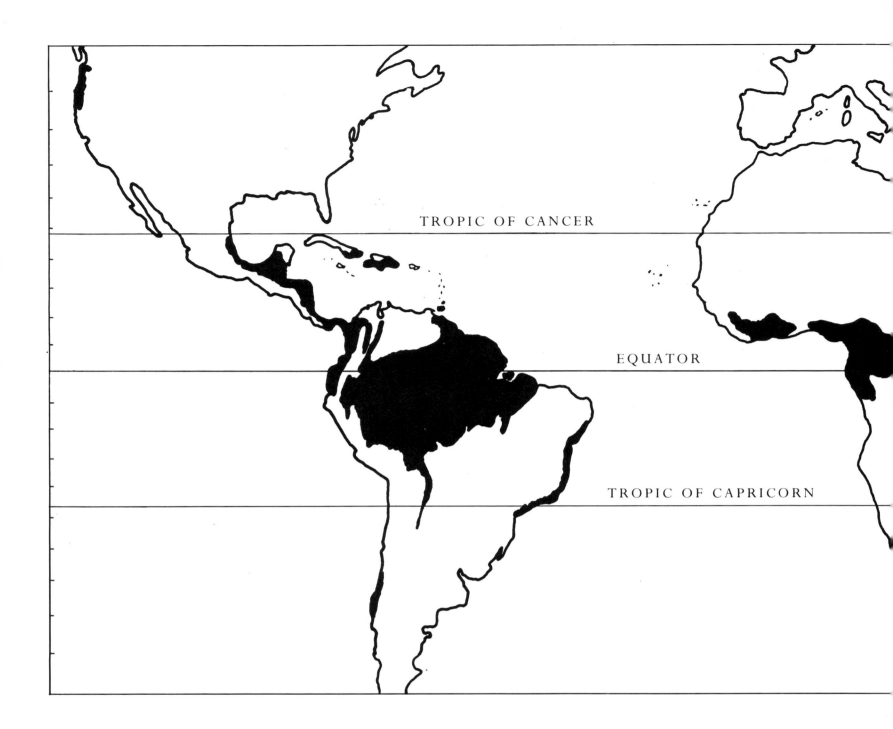

TROPIC OF CANCER

EQUATOR

TROPIC OF CAPRICORN

Preceding pages. *The cloud-capped summit of Mount Kinabalu is a splendid sight when viewed from over the top of the rain-forest canopy. Mount Kinabalu is one of the wettest places on earth, for it receives rain every day, with an annual average of 440 inches (11,000 mm).*

A substantial number of biologists have independently concluded that the rain forests of Amazonia, although continuous and apparently homogeneous today, were, in the distant past, subjected to a series of climatic hardships that reduced their area to a number of relatively small forest islands in a sea of grassland. It was within these forest refuges that the tropical rain-forest animals and plants survived long periods of aridity.

The rain forests of Africa, or Ethiopia as the biogeographers term Africa south of the Sahara, occur from the southern seaboard of West Africa into the Congo basin. To the north are the arid lands leading to the Sahara Desert, and to the south are the scrub forests and savannas of central South Africa. East of the Mitumba Mountains, within the irregular contours of Tanzania and Uganda, the rain forest is represented only by outlier islands within the parkland savannas.

Between twenty-five and twelve million years ago, the forests of Africa were much more extensive than they are today and were continuous with those of southern Asia, but increasing aridity favored grasslands at the expense of the forest. It was the opening up of the forest during the early

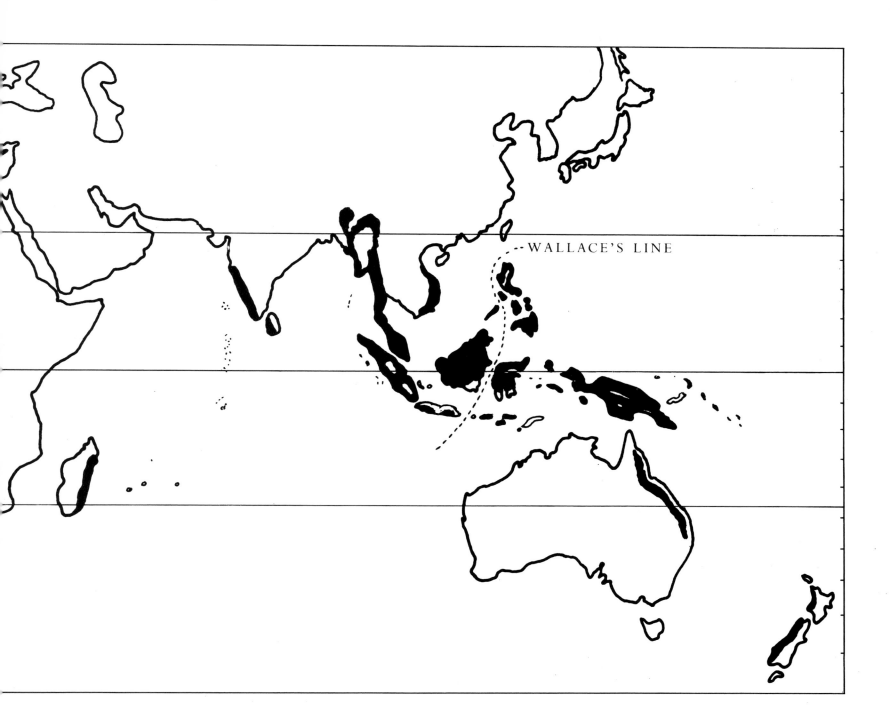

WALLACE'S LINE

Above. *On this map of the world, the contemporary natural distribution of the rain forests is shown in solid black. Notice that the maximum extension of the tropical rain forest is in northern Burma/eastern India, eastern Australia, and marginally in northern Argentina. The noteworthy temperate rain forests are in the Pacific northwest of the United States, western Chile, and New Zealand. The map is a modified version of Paul Richards's, 1952.*

part of this period that presented the opportunity for the development of grazing or browsing animals such as the zebra, wildebeest, and giraffe which are now so characteristic of the East African game reserves, along with their attendant predators, the lion, cheetah, and hyena.

It is again the periodic glaciations of the Pleistocene which have left their mark on the forests. According to Jonathon Kingdon, during the more recent colder and drier periods, the rain forest was fragmented into four distinct areas: the Upper Guinea refuge in the coastal region from Liberia to Ghana; the Cameroon refuge from southeast Nigeria to equatorial Guinea; the Central refuge in the heart of the Congo basin; and many point refuges in the mountains of Tanzania and Uganda. Although we see evidence of the unity of the African and Asian rain forests in the similarity of animals such as the elephants, rhinoceroses, and antelopes, the fragmentation of the African forests has allowed the development of species differences among some of the inhabitants of the old forest refuges.

Unlike continental islands, such as Trinidad, oceanic islands have never enjoyed a land connection with a nearby continent and have acquired all their plants and animals as

Preceding pages. The interior of the cloud forest is bright only during rather infrequent cloudless periods. Most cloud forests have fewer than ten cloudless days each year. The generally cool temperatures and poor light both contribute to the lowered productivity of these habitats when compared with forests that receive more sun. The effects of the specialized conditions can be seen here in Kota Kinabalu, Sabah, in that the trees are stunted, twisted, and heavily overgrown with epiphytes.

Opposite. The forests at 305 feet (1,000 m) at Cibodja in Java at first give the impression of being inundated with pendulous epiphytes, but closer inspection reveals that the effect is due to a conifer with drooping branches and leaves belonging to the Cupressaceae.

random introductions by sea or air. For many years, zoologists believed that the whole fauna of Madagascar had been obtained by way of chance arrivals on natural rafts broken off the banks of the Zambezi River. However, we now know that the island was once a part of Gondwanaland and has had its own native flora and fauna ever since parting company over fifty million years ago. However, the sudden appearance of hippopotamus bones in the fossil record long after Madagascar had become an island indicates that animals of that size can, indeed, arrive by a "sweepstakes" route. Personally, I still find the idea of hippopotamuses floating on rafts or swimming the five hundred miles (805 km) from Africa rather ludicrous, but one has to remember that then the distance may have been much less. A source of encouragement to a disbeliever is a report from an eyewitness who told me how he watched a small exhausted caiman alligator crawl off a log that had washed up on a beach off the island of Grenada. The nearest known locality for these animals is Trinidad, some 90 miles (145 km) to the south, but from a study of the ocean currents it seems more likely that the caiman had been rafted on a piece of debris from the banks of the Orinoco River in northeastern South America, a truly formidable distance of at least 150 miles (241 km).

Oceanic island communities usually have novel characteristics which set them apart from those of the mainland. The seeds of mainland plants may germinate on an offshore island in the absence of their natural herbivores, or animals may become established in the absence of their native predators and parasites. New relationships may be struck between species that have not met each other in their originating territories. A colony may be founded by a single pregnant female that is not typical of the mainland race from which it came, and so the island descendants may genuinely appear to be different. The rigors of the environment may favor particular features, such as small size, and so lead to the selection of dwarfs.

Whereas the South American rain forests are recently united fragments, the forests of Southeast Asia and the Indonesian islands of the Sunda Shelf are the remnants of a continent, comparable in size with the northern half of South America, which has become dissected by the higher levels of the interglacial oceans.

As long ago as 1876, Alfred Russel Wallace, the supreme naturalist, noticed that the animals of Indonesia could be divided into two groups and that each group inhabited a particular portion of that area, with the boundary lying along the channel between the islands of Celebes and Borneo. The northern group occupied Borneo, Java, Sumatra, and peninsular Malaya, while the southern animals were found in Celebes, New Guinea, and the northern tip of Australia. The interface between these two groups has become known as "Wallace's line." The explanation for the substantial differences between these groups of animals is clear to us now. The water channel on either side of Celebes is much deeper than those separating the other islands

and has, therefore, been an effective barrier to animal movements for a long time.

Those islands now separated by only shallow water were probably united by a land connection during the last glacial period, so enabling terrestrial animals to disperse widely. However, unexplained difficulties still remain. Can the substantial differences in the contemporary mammals and birds of these islands have arisen in so short a time?

The Malay peninsular islands and neighboring Indonesian islands seem to have occupied their present geographic position for over eighty million years, during which time the flora has changed from being principally coniferous to one that reflects the dominance of the flowering plants. This transition has been deduced from the record of fossil pollen and other plant parts, but although the climate seems to have been continuously humid, the composition of the flora has undergone several periods of very rapid change. We are reminded that although changes through geologic time are usually gradual, they do seem to be punctuated by catastrophic disturbances.

The forests of tropical Asia differ markedly from the forests of Africa and America in that they are dominated by a single family of trees, the Dipterocarpaceae. In neither of the other rain-forest regions is there such a preponderance of a single family of trees. However, the Americas do enjoy the almost unique possession of the Bromeliaceae, a family of plants to which the cultivated pineapple belongs and which most frequently grows on the branches of trees without any connection with the ground. Even an inexperienced botanist, dropped into the rain forest by parachute from a poorly navigated aircraft, would at least know on which continent he or she had landed as soon as it was light enough to see.

As overall precipitation declines and fires become more common, the trees thin out and form the parkland savannas that are typical of the game reserves of East Africa or the Guinea savannas of West Africa. The savannas characteristically have widely spaced trees with the intervening grass rising up to eight feet (2.4 m) before it is cut back by fire.

With increasing aridity the gallery forest becomes attenuated, the savanna trees become sparse and stunted, and the grasses are restricted to widely scattered bunches. The boundaries of the desert have been reached. The high daytime temperatures and low humidity prevent all but the most hardy animals from hunting for food during the day. Most larger animals burrow into the ground and emerge only during the cool of the night, when the relative humidity is higher and droplets of water can sometimes be harvested from the cool surfaces of the succulent desert plants. Water is at such a premium that it is hardly surprising to find that the plants here are all spiny, poisonous, or both, as a protection from ravenously hungry and thirsty herbivores.

Where the rain forest approaches the sea, there is a rapid change in the species composition, for few forest plants can withstand the high soil salinity caused by accumulations of windblown salt or from contamination of groundwater by the sea. The growth of most of the plants that occur is stunted to some extent. Worldwide, tropical beach lines are populated with palm trees where the soil is sandy and mangrove where it is muddy. Most commonly, the mud is derived from the weathering of inland granitic rocks and has been transported to the estuaries down the streams and rivers. Tropical deltas are almost always densely forested with mangrove.

To meet the challenge of tidal fluctuations, the mangroves have extensive rooting systems that originate above the high-water mark on the trunk and project as a pyramid of props which support the plant as well as serving as nutrient traps. The constant waterlogging of the roots necessitates unusual methods for the aeration of the root tissues, a problem which different mangrove species have overcome in different ways. Some mangroves have fingerlike outgrowths of the submerged roots which project up into the air, others have vertical kinks in their roots, which again project into the air in the manner of "knees." Because of the hazard of having their seeds washed out into unsuitable environments, mangrove plants germinate their seeds while still on the parent tree and drop their seedlings into the underlying mud in the form of a dart.

Wherever mangrove occurs, the protection offered by the densely interlocking roots and the abundance of waterborne nutrients flowing into the estuary assures a high population of small marine organisms. The mangrove is a tropical nursery for many fish species and other marine life, including some that are harvested for human food. The slow growth rate of mangrove and its extreme susceptibility to death by defoliation makes the destruction of the mangroves in parts of Vietnam a major ecological disaster. Man-made pollutants have also recently endangered mangrove communities in Florida and Puerto Rico.

Landward of the mangrove, and scattered throughout the rain forest wherever the land is subject to extensive flooding, there are areas of freshwater swamp. The vegetation is typically rich in palms equipped with root knees similar to those of the mangrove. The height of the knees gives a good indication of the level of the floodwaters, for the top of the knees must remain in the air to provide a surface for gas exchange with the tissues of the roots. The várzea forests of the floodplain of the Amazon are the most extensive forests of this type in the world.

From the seasonless lowland rain forest at sea level, the changes with increasing altitude are almost imperceptible up to about three thousand feet (920 m). There will be only a gradual reduction in the diversity of species, the overall height of the trees, the stratification of the canopy, and in the average size of individual leaves. The leaves may also tend to be less regular in outline and more commonly divided into leaflets.

These changes are mainly in response to decreasing temperature, for the overall rainfall may be just as great as at lower elevations. The average daily temperature

Following pages. (left) *These giant kapok trees (Ceiba pentandra: Bombacaceae) at Manaus on the Amazon in Brazil are remnants of the rain forest. If they had grown in such isolation since youth the branching would be much lower on the trunk. The tall, straight, unbranched trunk is characteristic of rain-forest trees grown under crowded conditions. Notice also the typical spherical crowns. This area has evidently been recently cleared of forest.*

(right) *At Horton Plains, Sri Lanka, the cloud forest is scrubby at the highest elevation and gradually gives way to grassland before yielding to bare rock at about seventy-five hundred feet (2,475 m). The contorted, gnarled, and mangy-looking tree in the foreground is typical of the cloud-forest habitat.*

decreases by 4°F (2°C) for every one-thousand-feet (305-m) increase in altitude, a decline that affects all organisms to some extent, for all biochemical reactions are temperature sensitive. Even the warm-blooded mammals and birds are affected, for with increasing cold they have to expend more energy in fueling their heat production in order to maintain a constant body temperature, and this requires that they eat more food. It is the night temperature that is most important, for some nocturnal animals may be unable to remain active if the nights are too cold. In addition, the evaporation of water from the leaf surface of plants can cool the leaf to a temperature several degrees below that recorded on a thermometer suspended in the air.

In many areas of the tropical world, the local conditions produce almost continuous dense cloud cover at about 3,000 to 5,000 feet (920 to 1,500 m), the exact altitude varying from place to place. Under these conditions of reduced light, cold but not freezing nights, and nearly year-round saturation humidity, we find the cloud forests of South and Central America and the mossy forests of Southeast Asia.

Even where the climatic conditions are insufficiently severe for the development of cloud forests, the reduced precipitation and lowered humidity inhibit the growth of many of the rain-forest species, and they are replaced by deciduous trees that shed their leaves during the dry season. These forests are much smaller in stature than the

Above. *The temperate rain forests of the western coast of South Island of New Zealand are frequently overlooked but they have all the features of the rain forest. Here, the dark interior is replete with herbaceous epiphytes.*

lower-altitude forests that they replace and may have only a single canopy layer. The understory is much more rich because of the weakened density and light-excluding ability of the canopy.

Eventually, at altitudes approaching ten to twelve thousand feet (3,000 to 3,600 m), the freezing night temperatures and sporadic rainfall inhibit the growth of trees completely and the vegetation gives way to stunted woody shrubs, grasses, and annual herbs. In different regions, these essentially alpine communities are termed paramo (South America), Afro-alpine (Africa), or Asia-alpine (Southeast Asia). Beyond these communities lie the lichens and the snow line.

In 1967, Leslie R. Holdridge, an eminent American ecologist, and his co-worker ecologists proposed a classification of the world's vegetation that would encompass elevation, latitude, rainfall, humidity, and average temperature. According to Holdridge, the wettest lowland rain forest has a mean annual temperature of 75°F (24°C), a rainfall above 320 inches (8,000 mm) each year, and a superhumid atmosphere. Increasing altitude takes one into premontane rain forest, where rainfall is below 320 inches, and then into lower montane rain forest, where the precipitation is annually at least 160 inches (4,000 mm) but temperatures fall as low as 54°F (12°C). The 60 to 80-inch (2,000- to 4,000-mm) rainfall belt is known as montane forest and is usually strongly seasonal.

At increasing latitude, a similar series of forests are encountered, but are termed subtropical (equal to premontane), warm temperate (equal to lower montane), and cool temperate (equal to premontane). Temperate rain forests are rare, the best-known example being the Douglas fir forests of the northwestern United States and those of southwestern New Zealand. At lower elevations in the tropics, decreasing precipitation is characteristic of lowland rain forest, through wet forest, moist forest, dry forest, and ultimately to the desert.

Our knowledge of the world's rain forests is sketchy, but the coarse-grained picture is clear. Perhaps because of more severe climatic perturbations in the past, the forests of the neotropics are the richest. There are no reliable data on species numbers which apply only to the rain forest, but the inventory of tropical plants exemplifies the situation. Ghillean Prance has recently summarized current knowledge and estimates that there are 155,000 known tropical flowering plants, of which 90,000 are American, 35,000 are Asian, and 30,000 are African. The proportions among the known fungi are similar, with 50,000 from the Americas and 20,000 from each of the other two areas. The ferns are less adequately known, but tropical America certainly has as many as either of the other two regions. These figures favor the Americas in spite of the fact that the fauna of Africa and Asia has been better collected than that of tropical America through more enlightened colonialism.

Above. *This coniferous rain forest in the Olympic National Park in coastal Washington State shows the massive development of herbaceous epiphytes, which are characteristic of temperate rain forests. In the tropics, the epiphytes are perennial and woody.*

Following pages. *From the botanical gardens at Lae in New Guinea, this stormy sunset could have provided inspiration to a musician, painter, photographer, or even a science writer.*

From Close Up

The jungles of Tarzan and Errol Flynn have cast images of the tropical rain forest that are difficult to erase. The forests of the movie set are, for logistical reasons, rarely far from centers of commerce and have been altered by centuries of human activity. The tangled lattice of vines and the preeminence of bamboo are the hallmarks of disturbance. The mature rain forest is incompatible with human greed, so few examples of virgin forest are to be found near dense human populations.

The jungle image has been further reinforced by the pictures and descriptions brought back by explorers who navigated the equatorial waterways. From a canoe, the river is bounded by a solid wall of green that rises far above the water. But the riverbank is the "edge" of the forest and, where undisturbed, is the only edge the forest has. It is hardly surprising that there is a superabundance of herbs, shrubs, and climbers at the only place where the full force of the sunlight reaches the ground.

Mere humans are overwhelmed by the grandeur, tranquillity, and presence of the rain forest. Like fluted columns of an enormous natural cathedral, the tree trunks tower toward the heavens and fuse with the sculptured foliage of the canopy. The little light that reaches the forest floor has been reflected a dozen times from as many leaves, and with the reds and blues withdrawn the yellowish green diffusion transforms human figures into ghouls.

To the tourist, perhaps the most striking feature of the rain forest is the uniformity, for everywhere you look, in whichever forest you are in, the foliage appears consistently monotonous. With the exception of the multipointed fan palms, the leaves of the forest trees are usually less than six inches long (15 cm), dark green with a glossy upper surface, leathery in texture, and of elliptical shape with the tips drawn to a point. Among the better-known temperate plants, the laurel most closely resembles the typical rain-forest tree leaf. The usual shape for the leaves of climbers is that of a heart or arrowhead, again with the tip narrowed to a point.

Aided by the glossy upper surface, the pointed leaf tips, or "drip tips" as they are known, are thought to benefit the plant in one or perhaps all of three different ways, each of which depends upon the rapid run off of surface water. First, the accelerated drying may inhibit the attachment of algae and other encrusting organisms, which might otherwise gain a purchase on the leaf surface and find the abundance of moisture conducive to growth. Second, the quick run off may prevent excessive cooling by evaporation of surface water which, if allowed to remain, would lower the temperature of the inner tissues of the leaf and slow the activities of the living cells. Third, the presence of the surface water may block the normal evaporation of water from the pores in the leaf surface and disturb the transport of dissolved minerals through the body of the plant. This last reason seems immediately questionable, for studies on the leaves of temperate plants have shown that in most cases the evaporative pores are more numerous on the lower surface of the leaf. Whichever of these reasons, if any, is the correct one, there is no doubt that drip tips do accelerate the removal of the water.

Most people who enjoy houseplants are already familiar with rain-forest leaves, for most of the shade-loving foliage plants cultivated for interior decoration have tropical rain-forest origins. Some good examples are *Monstera, Philodendron, Hoya,* and *Dieffenbachia.*

It is not only the foliage which is responsible for the uniformity of the rain forest, for the high humidity of the forest interior makes a thick waterproof bark superfluous, so most trees have a thin bark of rather consistent appearance. The richly fissured and interesting bark of the temperate walnut or oak is not to be found here. The only major sources of relief from monotony are the spines of such trees as the silk-cotton (*Ceiba pentandra*), but outside Southeast Asia even trunk spines are more common in the drier regions. Only the palms have true individuality on their trunks, for they each bear the everlasting scars of the leaves of their youth.

A source of great frustration to taxonomic botanists is that the appearance of both the leaves and the bark of tropical trees changes with advancing maturity. Add to that the difficulty of obtaining flowers and fruits, or even foliage, from the one-hundred-foot-tall canopy and the problems are obvious. It is largely for logistical reasons that the rain-forest trees are more poorly represented in museum collections than any other type of tropical vegetation.

The trees planted in botanical gardens can be useful in providing specimens for identification and description, but can be misleading with regard to overall shape and growth habit. The forest tree competes vigorously with its neighbors and has a growth pattern that demands rapid height gain at relatively low light intensities. The same tree planted to decorate a college campus is not faced with such adversity. It is grown in isolation from competition for light, and may have a root cover of grass or other herbs. Instead of having to compete with other trees and then finally take its place among highest levels in the canopy, the isolated tree will branch very early in its life and comparatively near the ground, producing a much broader and shallower canopy than its forest counterpart. Floral characters will be true to type, but leaf size and shape, as well as bark texture and overall growth habit, may be quite atypical.

A mature tree left standing after the rest of the forest has been felled will retain its mature shape and stand with its crown atop a majestic, limbless trunk. The same tree left as a sapling would have a much deeper canopy arising much lower on the trunk. This situation is not novel; the same remarks apply to temperate trees. The "spreading chestnut tree" of poetic fame had undoubtedly enjoyed many years of growth unencumbered by competition from its neighbors.

Francis Hallé, of the Institut de Botanique at Montpellier in France, has long been interested in the architecture of tropical trees. Hallé contends that the rain

Preceding pages. (top left) *On cool, humid mornings, many herbaceous plants exude droplets of water from pores around the edges of their leaves. This water secretion, known as guttation, is clearly visible in these leaves of* Baphia nitida *(Papilionaceae) in Ghana.*

(bottom left) *The fruiting bodies of this species of* Nectria *from Ghana belie the extent of the fungus's threadlike hyphae within the wood. Fungi are perhaps the most important decomposers in the humid, warm tropics.*

(bottom right) *These fungi on a still-erect tree trunk in Amazonas, Brazil, are not the cause of the tree's death, for the tree has to be dying or under severe stress before the fungi can become established. The largest of the fruiting bodies illustrated is about one inch across.*

(right) *Miniature parachutes? No, just the fruiting bodies of the fungus* Maresmius *from Tingo María, Peru.*

forests of the different continents are similar in their branching patterns and that tropical rain-forest trees rarely have more than four orders of branching, which means that if a terminal twig is traced back to the main trunk there will have been only three forks. Temperate trees usually have five to eight orders of branching and therefore seem to have a much finer texture to their canopy.

Our present knowledge of the rain forest has been obtained only by superlative effort, for the visiting botanist is faced with a formidable task. How can the rain forest be studied? For, once inside, the observer is a prisoner. How can one sample vegetation a hundred feet beyond one's grasp? How are large fruits to be preserved when so far from camp? There are no easy answers. Sadly, the only way to study the forest requires that we destroy a piece of it. A typical area is selected, the trees are labeled, mapped, and then felled, one by one. Each tree is measured and all the plants are identified and arranged in size classes. With these data, a profile diagram is constructed which portrays the arrangement of the living trees and their associated vegetation. The minimally acceptable size of a sample would be 200 feet by 25 feet (60 x 7.5 m) and in order to avoid the criticism that the chosen site was atypical, a second sample of similar size is also needed to show consistent results. The labor required to fell such an area is truly awesome.

However, stimulated by the example set by the breathtaking climbs of lichenologist William Denison and his associates in the temperate rain forests, other intrepid arboreers are now exploring the canopies of standing tropical trees. Previously, beyond personal endurance tests such as that of Ivan T. Sanderson, who spent two weeks at a height of 120 feet (37 m) in the crown of a forest tree in Nicaragua, and observations from steel towers of similar height in the forests of East and West Africa, canopy data were limited to the study of semi-isolated trees, hurricane damage, felled transects, and the use of binoculars from the ground. With equipment designed by Donald Perry, of the University of California at Los Angeles, an investigator of moderate athletic skill but unusual courage can now climb into the canopy of any tall forest tree using only equipment that can be carried on his or her back. We are on the threshold of a period of enlightenment.

So, a broad view of a rain forest shows a canopy of tree crowns widely separated from the forest floor by a space some fifty feet (15.2 m) deep. The crowns themselves form a jigsaw mosaic that catches almost all the sunlight. The tallest trees emerge between their underlings and spread their mushroom-shaped crowns over those of their neighbors. These emergent trees are usually between 150 and 180 feet tall (45 to 55 m), but exceptional ones may approach 300 feet (90 m). They are the giants of the rain forest but are widely scattered and are termed "A level" by forest ecologists. Beneath the emergent crowns lie the irregularly spherical crowns of the "B level," which reach from between 60 and 90 feet (20 to 30 m) from the ground. The foliage of these trees may not be touching, but their branches are so densely wired together by a lattice of vines that they form a virtually continuous layer. The light that filters past the A and B layers is trapped by the "C level," consisting of trees with elongate conical crowns that fit loosely between those of the B level at a height of between 25 and 45 feet (7.5 to 15 m). This intricate interlocking network of foliage ensures that only from 3 to 15 percent of the sunlight penetrates the upper canopy. The illumination that finally penetrates to the forest floor may be as little as 1 percent of the sunlight beaming down on the canopy above.

The forest floor is sparsely populated with small plants, for the light that directly penetrates the canopy produces a dappled pattern of flecks which, even though each fleck may be one hundred times brighter than the background illumination, move with the rotation of the earth. Rarely is any part of the soil surface illuminated strongly enough or long enough to support living ground cover. Only when some accident has opened up the canopy will there be a covering of fernlike *Selaginella,* true ferns, herbs, or grass. The majority of the surface of the forest floor is concealed by fallen leaves, twigs, and branches in various stages of decomposition. The nutrients of the rain-forest soils are never far below the surface, so the rooting systems of many trees are partially exposed. The roots of even large trees may be no deeper than eighteen inches (.5 m) below the surface. The permanent presence of the tree roots in the upper layers of the soil, where they compete with terrestrial herbs for nutrients, is an additional reason why the ground cover is so scanty. The only understory plants that are common are climbers, dwarf palms, and a variety of saplings. The life history of these saplings is most unusual, for if the seeds survive predation, they spend one or two years as seedlings and then grow rapidly to a height of about 12 to 15 feet (3.5 to 4.5 m). At this height they wait, sometimes for years, for the appearance of a light gap in the canopy brought about by a catastrophe to a near neighbor.

Standing in awe and contemplating the vastness of the rain forest, one is struck not only by the silence but also by the stillness. There is not a breath of wind. It is only in the light gaps, where the forest canopy has been opened up by the death of a large tree, that the sun can warm the forest floor and generate convection currents in the air. Flowers born under the canopy have no chance of being wind pollinated, so they depend on insects, bats, or birds. It is, perhaps, because the understory is so open, while the lower canopy is so dense, that many rain-forest trees have elected to bear their flowers directly on their trunks and not, as we in temperate climates have come to expect, on their terminal twigs and shoots. Cauliflory, as this condition is termed, renders the flowers much more visible to potential pollinators than they would be if they were buried in the foliage. Outside the evergreen rain forest, many seasonally deciduous trees have met the challenge of advertising their flowers by restricting their canopy flowering to the dry season when there are no leaves to obscure the display. In the evergreen forest there is no such opportunity, for

Opposite. *Although the bark of rain-forest trees is characteristically smooth, few are as colorful as* Eucalyptus nadoniana *(Myrtaceae), the silk tree from New Guinea.*

Above. Dracaena deremensis *(Liliaceae) from tropical Africa is popular with horticulturists, who have bred many named varieties. The horizontal bands on the trunk are the scars of leaves that have been shed.*

Left. *The relationship between the leaves and the trunk is clearly visible on this dragon tree* (Dracaena ellenbeckian).

Opposite. (top) *In this stylized rain-forest profile diagram, notice the very tall, relatively unbranched trunks with buttresses at the base of the larger trees. Notice also the layering of the canopy into the mushroom-shaped emergent A-level crowns, the closely packed spherical crowns of the B level, and the lower C-level conical crowns. Saplings are growing underneath the forest canopy. Individual forests may vary considerably from this generalized plan, depending on local climatic and soil conditions and species composition of the forest.*

(bottom) *The spreading canopy of this saman tree (Samanea saman) casts its shade over half an acre of the University of the West Indies campus at St. Augustine in Trinidad. The tree has witnessed many changes during its more than one hundred fifty years: the site was a tropical-disease hospital at the end of the nineteenth century, became the Imperial College of Tropical Agriculture in the 1920s, and the Trinidad campus of the University of the West Indies in 1960.*

although each leaf ultimately becomes senescent and is shed after about a year or so, it is a continuous process without seasonality.

Looking at the tree trunks at eye level one cannot avoid noticing that many of the larger trees have their trunks drawn out into massive ridges near the base. The function of these buttresses is much debated. Paul Richards, author of *The Tropical Rain Forest,* suggested that they were specializations to transport soil water in a way that would not interfere with other root activities. Engineers, such as Kenneth Henwood, point to a response to the stresses and strains imposed on tall trees with shallow rooting systems, particularly if the crowns grow asymmetrically and become unbalanced. Indeed it is true that, mechanically, the exaggeratedly stellate cross-section of the trunk would resist uprooting, but the canopy of the rain forest is so dense, and tree crowns interdependent, that one can question just how great the lateral forces on a single tree can be. Under hurricane-force winds, is the whole forest being bent sideways or does the eye of the storm place extreme force on individual trees? Judging from the damage caused by tornadoes in the United States, the latter seems more likely and it may be against such random occurrences that buttresses have been developed. However, I have observed that hurricanes usually snap off the crowns of the emergent and B-level trees, leaving the trunks to rot and become overgrown with vines. Their buttress roots seem to do little more than determine the way in which they die and afford little protection against death itself.

Another feature running counter to the mechanical-strength hypothesis is that not all trees develop buttresses in situations when they would be expected. Some trees have well-developed buttresses, whereas other individuals of the same species in an apparently similar locality do not. Alan Smith, working in Dominica, found a correlation between buttress development and thinness of bark and postulated that the ridging increases the surface area available for the exchange of oxygen and carbon dioxide in regions where the soils are poorly aerated. This hypothesis is consistent with the observation of Richards that buttresses are more common in trees growing in wetter areas. Thicker-barked trees, it is argued, would find the manufacturing of so much bark too expensive to be justified and hence rarely develop buttresses. Certainly these buttresses can be very impressive structures, for they may rise thirty feet (9.1 m) before blending into the cylindrical contours of the trunk, or still be visible on roots a similar distance away from the bole.

The idea of roots being visible at eye level is quite foreign to a temperate-zone visitor to the tropical rain forest. But there they are. Palm trees are particularly susceptible to being uprooted by high winds and many species are characteristic of flood-prone areas. These problems of stability have been met by initiating lateral roots from points high on the trunk and developing them sideways until they reach the ground. Although the growth of the trees as a whole is fairly slow, the growth of these

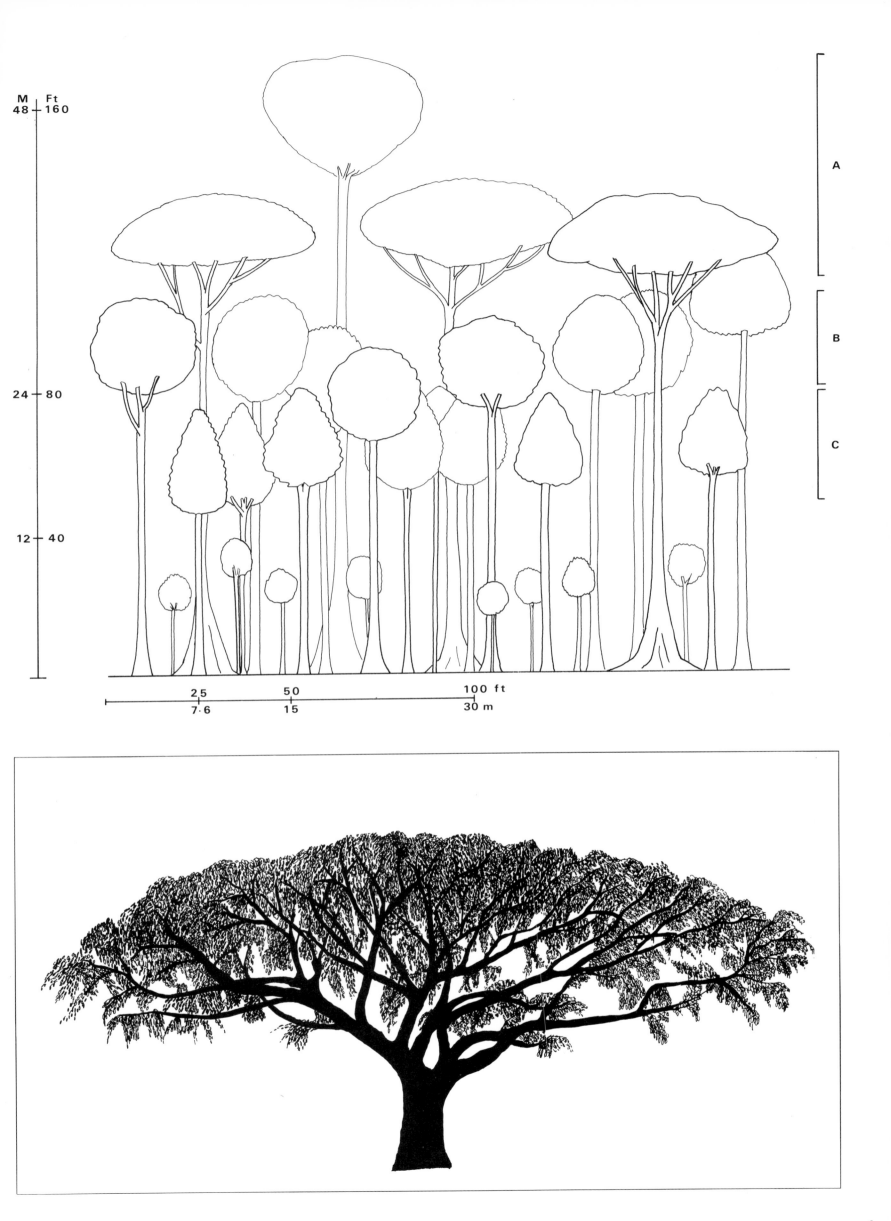

M Ft
48 — 160

24 — 80

12 — 40

A

B

C

25
7·6

50
15

100 ft

30 m

Left. *This red silk-cotton* (Bombax malabaricum: *Bombacaceae*) *from Indochina is protected by coarse thorns. The chlorophyll in the surface tissues shows that this is a young stem, but the thorns will persist throughout development and are prominent on the trunks of mature 100-foot-tall trees.*

Above. *The smooth bark of a rain-forest tree in Sri Lanka forms the substrate for a climbing* Ficus diverformis *(Moraceae). The bark is already encrusted with lichens. Notice that the main stem of the climber grows straight up toward the peak light intensity. No energy is wasted in lateral growth.*

Right. *The cacao tree* (Theobroma cacao) *bears the mature cacao pod on the oldest part of the trunk. With its probable native origin on the eastern slopes of the Andes, cacao has been cultivated in Central America for perhaps as long as two thousand years and was believed by the Indians to be of divine origin. The word "cocoa" is used for manufactured products, such as chocolate, while "cacao" is reserved for the plant.*

aerial roots can be rapid, for extensions of twenty-eight inches (70 cm) in a month have been recorded. These prop roots, if relatively short, or stilt roots, if relatively long (as in *Pandanus,* the so-called screw pine), are a characteristic feature of tropical palms growing in shallow, wet soils. The exposed roots may also serve to trap ground litter and flood debris and thus add to the nutrients in the vicinity of their roots.

Massive trunks, buttress roots, surface roots, stilt roots, prop roots—everywhere you look there is wood, all seeming rather uniform. The woodiness is real but the uniformity is not. A botanist would sum up the tropical rain forest in these two words: woodiness and diversity.

Woodiness allows grasses to grow to a height of sixty feet (18 m) in the form of bamboos, ferns which can become as tall as temperate trees, and climbers which smother the grandest trees and develop stems as thick as a human thigh. These excesses are characteristic of the tropical rain forest. However, large size itself is not peculiar to the tropical rain forest, for the coniferous rain forests of the western United States have trees that are taller than those of the tropics. In fact, the tallest measured tree in the world (396 feet, 120 m) was a sequoia from California. Epiphytes, plants that grow on other plants but derive nutrients from the air and rain, are characteristic of the tropical rain forest but not confined to it. They are sometimes common in temperate climates, notably in the southeastern and northwestern United States, though woody epiphytes are confined to the tropics.

Only a botanist with technical knowledge can fully appreciate the enormous diversity of species growing in a tropical rain forest. Whereas a temperate woodland in the eastern United States would have between 15 and 20 tree species, with only 2 or 3 such as oak, hickory, or beech being abundant, a similar area of tropical rain forest may have more than 100 species, none of which is conspicuously more common than any other. Unless they require special and geographically restricted soil conditions, the individuals of each species are usually widely scattered. It is not rare for the individuals of a single species to be separated by over half a mile. However, a few species, such as *Grewia coriacea* in West Africa, may be found in clumps because they have arisen by regrowth out of the trunk of a fallen parent. This situation is not to be confused with the "nurse logs" of the Washington rain forest in which a fallen Douglas fir rots and forms an eminently suitable germination medium for the seeds of the same species. However, although different in origin, both of these growth patterns result in a line of trees which is so straight that it is difficult to believe that they were not planted by hand.

There is controversy among tropical botanists over the extent to which mature trees inhibit the growth of their own seedlings beneath their canopies. Although from the tree's point of view it would seem desirable to exclude the possibility of being in competition with its own offspring, the system would also determine that the parental place in the sun was inevitably yielded to a member of another species. The probable outcome of the debate will be, as so often has been the case, that no generalization of wide applicability can be made. There are, however, some situations that are difficult to explain. For example, there are forests in Malaya in which nearly all the saplings waiting for their chance to break through the canopy are of species that are rare in the canopy under which they grow. Where did the seeds from which these saplings germinated come from? How long can seeds remain viable in the soil without germinating? Where are the seedlings of the mature trees? Are we witnessing long-term changes in the species composition of the forest? Is this valid evidence for lack of stability in tropical rain-forest systems?

These are just some of the questions being addressed by tropical biologists Tim Whitmore and Peter Ashton. Whatever the answers to those questions turn out to be, there is no doubt that the tropical rain forest operates on a very different plan from that of temperate forests. From close up, we see the differences expressed in woodiness and diversity, but the real difference is more fundamental than that—it involves the energy forces that drive the whole system.

Following pages. (left) *A common feature of understory tropical rain-forest plants is the bearing of flowers and fruit directly on the woody trunk. This example of cauliflory is* Phaleria capitata *from Bogor, Java.*

(right) *The cauliflorous papaya, or pawpaw* (Carica papaya), *has never been found in the wild but probably originated in southern Mexico or Costa Rica. Even though it is widely cultivated in the moist, humid tropics, its method of pollination is still not completely understood. Because of difficulties in transport, most pawpaw fruits are consumed locally. The meat tenderizer papain, prepared from the dried latex of the immature fruits, is exported to the United States.*

Above. *The enormous size that can be attained by buttress roots is shown by this* Miaoberlinia biauleata *from Zingena-Yabassi in Cameroon. This tree was exposed when the surrounding forest was cut down.*

Right. *The pandanus palm (*Pandanus *sp.) is famous for its stilt roots, which support the tree from damage by high winds and allow it to grow to great height. These plants are known as screw pines, though they are not pines.*

Below. *Stilt roots are common in rain-forest trees in families other than the Palmae and Pandanaceae, although those families most commonly display them. This palm from Amazonas has an abundance of hiding places for small animals among its stilt roots.*

Opposite. *These colorful stilt roots belong to a ginger plant (*Hornstedtia *sp.) in Sabah.*

Right. *One of the more unexpected features of the tropical rain forest is the presence of giant ferns of treelike dimensions. This* Cyathea *in a New Caledonian rain forest at 4,250 feet (1,300 m) is typical of the tree ferns, some of which may reach 60 feet (18.5 m) and have a trunk diameter of 12 inches (30 cm) or more.*

Center. *Although sometimes known as the peacock fern because of its stunning color,* Selaginella wildenovii *is more closely related to the mosses. This species is widely distributed in Southeast Asia, where it grows in the deep shade of the rain forest. The intense blue coloration is thought to provide efficient light capture at low light intensities.*

Bottom. *Newly opened leaves of both temperate and tropical plants are rich in anthocyanin pigments and are often red or purple in color. Explanations for this phenomenon range from protection from excessive ultraviolet light (before the green chlorophyll has had time to become synthesized) to protection from insects which are cued in only to green as a color for potential food. Notice on this example of a passion flower (Passifloraceae) from Manaus, Brazil, the tightly coiled tendril in the foreground.*

Opposite. *(top) This* Coccothrinax *from Cuba illustrates one of the many beautiful palm-leaf shapes.*

(bottom) The unopened leaves of this Blechnum *fern (Polypodiaceae) from Sri Lanka resemble the hairspring of a watch. When they uncurl, they will have opened to their mature size. The small bright green pads are densely covered with stomatal pores for rapid exchange of carbon dioxide and oxygen, a feature that allows the leaves to grow rapidly while they are opening.*

Following pages. *The regularly arranged brown spheres on the underside of this fern leaf* (Alsophila sinuata) *from Sri Lanka contain billions of spores. Dry atmosphere stimulates the explosive release of the spores into the wind, where they may be blown completely around the world. On reaching a suitable site, each spore attempts to grow into a tiny plant complete with sperm- and egg-producing structures.*

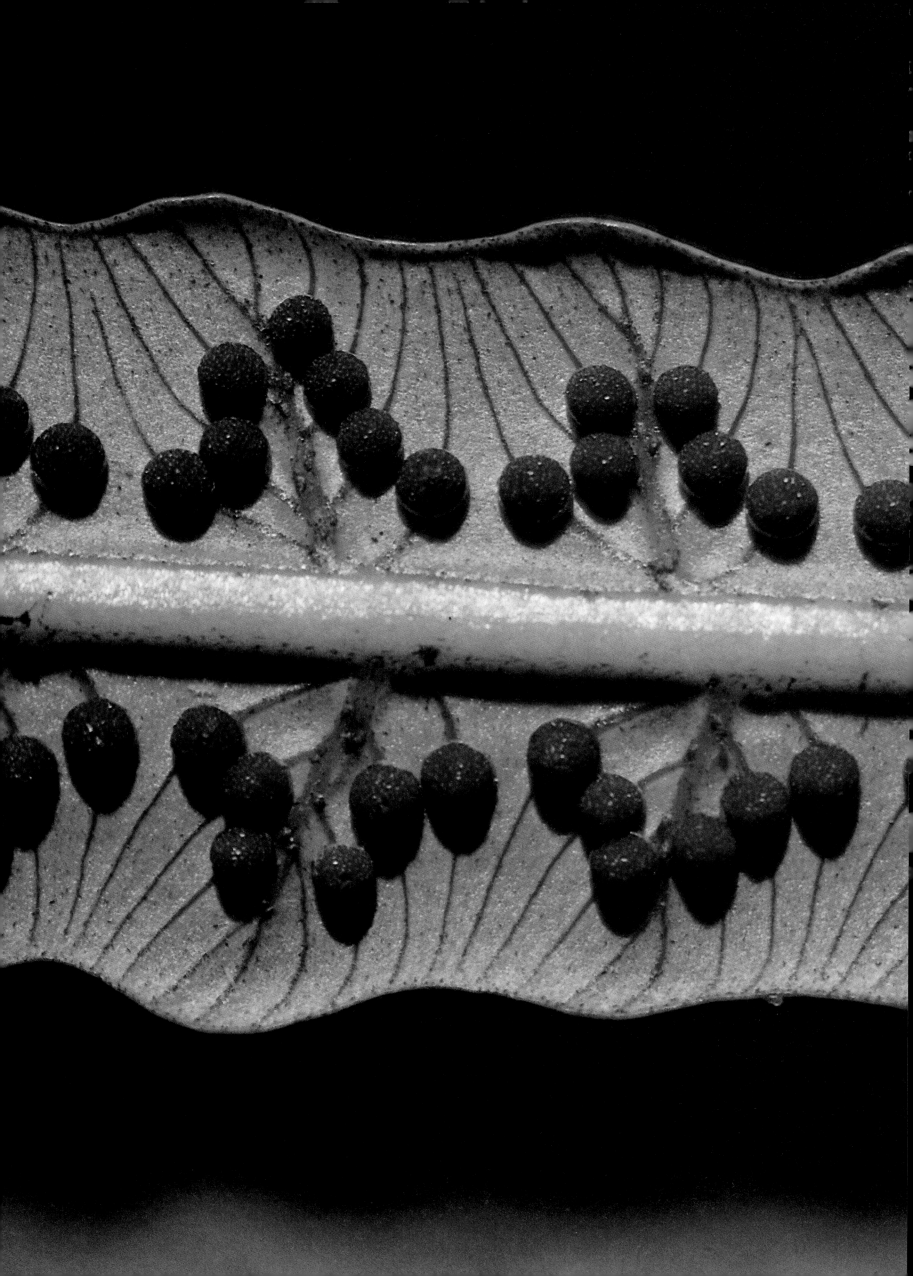

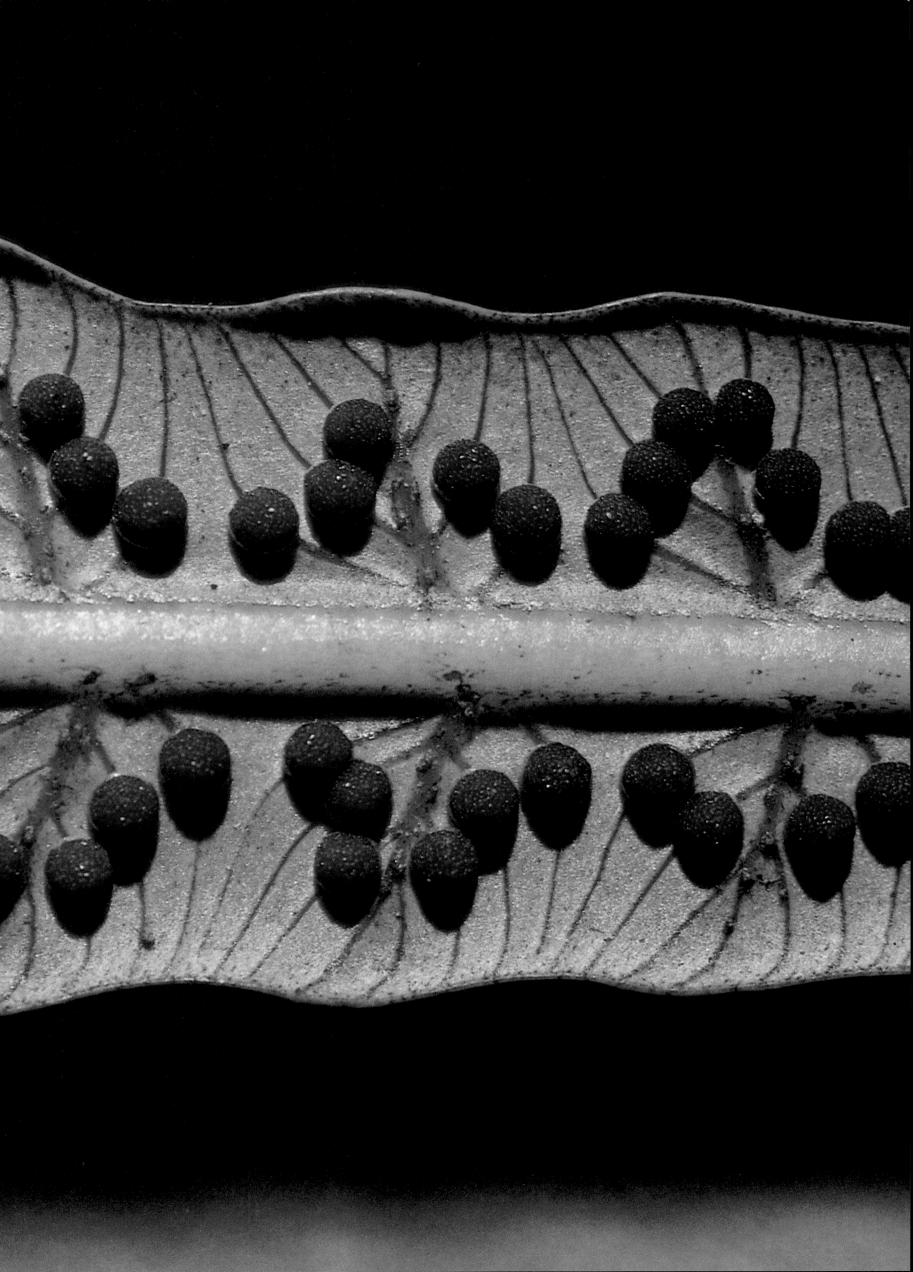

Driving Forces

The tropical rain forest is a classic case of a community feeding on itself! Because of the high day-long and year-round temperatures, biological activity proceeds apace. No sooner has a leaf, fruit, or animal corpse fallen to join the litter layer on the forest floor than fungi or bacteria begin to digest it. The death of the bacteria and fungi releases the nutrients back into the soil, where they are quickly taken up by the roots of a plant. The key to the understanding of the tropical rain forest is to appreciate the extraordinarily rapid turnover rate of the litter layer. Nutrients are withdrawn from the soil almost immediately after they have arrived.

Animals, by definition, eat other organisms, either living or dead, and so obtain their nutrients in a prepared form with most of the work of chemical synthesis already completed. Plants, on the other hand, make their own food materials from carbon dioxide in the air, and water and minerals from the soil. The assembly of complex chemicals requires energy, which is provided by the sun and harnessed by the process of photosynthesis.

The radiant energy from the sun has been our principal driving force for the past five billion years, and the pundits of astronomy predict that it will be with us for at least another five. Except for frequent fluctuations, the sun has increased its output substantially since the earth was formed and is shining more brightly now than it ever has before. We are directly aware of the existence of the sun because the retinas of our eyes are sensitive to one group of the relatively few bands of wavelength that are able to penetrate the earth's atmosphere. Collectively, these visible wavelengths produce the effect of "white" light, and it is components of white light that drive photosynthesis.

Robin Hill began our modern understanding of photosynthesis in England in 1937, but it has been only during the last decade that the details have become known with confidence. The key to the process is the catalyst chlorophyll, a tadpole-shaped molecule arranged around a single atom of magnesium which has the unique ability to trap a proportion of the sunlight that strikes it. We find chlorophyll in all the green structures that are exposed to sunlight, principally the leaves and terminal shoots. Chlorophyll seems to have existed for at least two billion years, for its decomposition products have been found in rocks containing algae of that age.

Although 75 to 80 percent of the sunlight falling on a leaf is absorbed, only about 10 percent of it is actually captured by chlorophyll and put to work for the plant; the remainder is either reflected at the leaf surface or converted into heat. The long red and short blue wavelengths of visible light are absorbed more readily by chlorophyll than the medium wavelengths, most of which are reflected and upon entering our eye produce the effect we recognize as green. Hence, green leaves and other green plant parts can readily be identified as sites of photosynthesis.

Photosynthesis is a two-part reaction. First, the incoming sunlight is trapped and its energy used partly to split water into its two atomic components, hydrogen and oxygen, and partly to drive the chemical reaction that follows. Second, the hydrogen and atmospheric carbon dioxide are passed through a series of exchanges, known as the Calvin-Benson cycle, in order to assemble molecules of the sugar glucose. Clearly, the first reaction can take place only during the daytime, whereas the second can take place in either the light or dark as long as the supply of hydrogen and carbon dioxide lasts.

Glucose consists of carbon, hydrogen, and oxygen in the proportions of 1:2:1. The carbon and oxygen are derived from carbon dioxide, which makes up 0.04 percent of the earth's atmosphere, and the hydrogen is obtained from water in the soil. The splitting of water into hydrogen and oxygen by the first reaction results in the release of oxygen. A popular view among modern biologists is that almost all the oxygen in the earth's atmosphere (20 percent) has been derived from photosynthesis over the past two billion years.

The glucose made by photosynthesis is moved through the plant to locations where it is needed, either as a basic building block for more complex substances or as a source of energy to drive reactions. The energy is released from glucose by a process known as cellular respiration, which returns the carbon dioxide to the atmosphere and synthesizes a modest amount of water for the plant. In essence, cellular respiration is photosynthesis in reverse, but it is carried out continuously by all living cells, both animal and plant. As only chlorophyll can harness the sun's radiant energy, the pigment is deposited exclusively in those parts of the plant, such as leaves and apical stems, which can gain good exposure. The plant's constant problem is to ensure that these photosynthetic surfaces compete successfully with those of their neighbors for a profitable place in the sunlight.

Because the sunlight striking the earth's atmosphere above the equator does so at right angles to the surface of the earth, and not tangentially as it does near the poles, the intensity of the light falling on the tropics is greater than elsewhere. Thus, it is not surprising that we find the greatest productivity in the tropics and therefore the greatest weight (biomass) of living plant material per acre.

However, light alone is not enough, for during the trapping of the sunlight by chlorophyll water is required as a source of the hydrogen that serves as an energy carrier. In the tropics, in spite of the abundance of light energy and favorable high temperatures, it is the availability of water that determines the type of vegetation which prevails. The need for water is twofold: not only is it essential for photosynthesis, but it is required as a vehicle for the absorption of nutrients by the roots and for general transportation within the plant. The upward movement of water through the stem or trunk is governed principally by the evaporation of water from the aerial parts of the plant, a process known as transpiration.

The tropical rain forest is a mirage of luxuriance. The ingredients for photosynthesis are in abundance but soil nutrients are usually scarce. Heavy rainfall, rich in dissolved

Above. *The* Victoria regia *and* V. cruziana *water lilies have enjoyed fame since Victorian times. The size to which water-lily leaves grow depends on the species and the light intensity. The stronger the light, the smaller the leaf is at maturity. The largest* V. regia *leaves measure about six feet (2 m) in diameter. Notice the forest litter lying on the leaves. The surrounding aquatic is the water hyacinth (*Eichhornia crassipes*), which, although a native of Brazil, has been spread by humans to all parts of the tropical world. The lands to the sides of this river are flooded for almost half the year; these are the várzea lands of Brazil.*

Right. *In open areas of the forest where light can penetrate to ground level, the herbaceous flora is lush and elegant. This clearing at Tjibodas in Java has a deep carpet of* Eupatorium *(Compositae).*

carbon dioxide from the atmosphere, leaches out the nutrients in the soil and flushes them into the rivers; those remaining are often chemically bound to clay particles in the soil and are not readily available for uptake by forest plants. How, then, is the luxuriance supported?

Initially, soil nutrients are derived from the decomposition of parent rock beneath the subsoil by the erosive action of wind, rain, and to a lesser extent the acids that result from the action of lightning in the atmosphere. The flooding of streams and rivers is the most powerful dispersive agent of nutrients in the form of silt, hence the floodplains of rivers have become prime sites for agriculture. In some localities the actions of volcanoes and winds have made a substantial contribution to the formation of soils.

Of all the substances in the soil that are needed for plant growth, nitrogen is the one which is the most commonly deficient. Ironically, although 80 percent of our air is nitrogen, only a relatively small number of blue-green algae and soil bacteria have developed a method of acquiring it directly. Most of the rest of the plant world has to absorb nitrogen as soluble nitrate in the soil which has resulted from the microbial decay of dead organisms and animal waste. The Leguminosae, however, is a fortunate family of plants, for 90 percent of its members have established a mutualistic relationship with species of the soil bacterium *Rhizobium,* which can trap atmospheric nitrogen. In exchange for providing housing in root nodules and a supply of sugars, the bacteria pass on nitrates synthesized from the atmosphere. There is now active research going on to develop strains of agricultural crops belonging to other families that can also utilize these beneficial bacteria. On the death of the legume, the amount of nitrate returned to the soil is considerable and justifies the plowing in of leguminous crops such as peas and beans in times of low commercial price or after the harvest of the fruits.

A factor that is only just beginning to be understood is the special relationship between the roots of many tropical-forest trees and specific soil fungi. These mycorrhizal fungi form a network over and into the surface of the roots of many forest trees and are thought to provide the roots with an accelerated flow of nutrients from the soil. In exchange, the tree roots supply sugars to amplify the energy budget of the fungus. The introduction of pine trees into Puerto Rico and Australia was met with success only when the soil was inoculated by specific soil fungi which were present in the homeland soils. In cooperation with the mycorrhizae, the trees grew rapidly. Many ecologists have remarked upon the superabundance of fungi in the soils of the Amazon rain forest and believe that many of them may have established mycorrhizal associations. The intimate relationship between the fungus and the tree may well be essential for each and is probably responsible for the extremely rapid pickup of soil nutrients in tropical-forest soils. This area of investigation has great potential for tropical ecologists and will undoubtedly have a broad impact on future agricultural research.

In a recent paper, Carl F. Jordan and his colleagues have shown that dissolved calcium, sulfur, and phosphorus are scavenged from rainwater as it falls through the tropical-forest canopy, probably by lichens and algae. This input of nutrients is an important contribution to a system with poor soil fertility. Comparisons with the temperate rain forest of the Olympic peninsula in Washington State show that the water reaching the forest floor there is richer in calcium and phosphorus than rain that falls on the canopy, which suggests that the scavenging ability is a tropical adaptation to impoverished soils.

Tropical soils are usually rather porous and allow rapid draining. With high levels of rainfall and rapid decomposition of litter, the nutrients are either in the surface layer, where active decomposition is taking place, or on their way to the sea. Hence, we find that the roots of most tropical-forest trees are shallow and may even be visible above the surface of the ground.

Vast areas of the tropics are covered with a deep layer of red soil that is rich in the oxides of aluminum and iron. These laterite soils are highly acidic and therefore do not hold nutrients well. However, their chief handicap is that if allowed to become hot, as they do if the overlying vegetation is removed, then the soil becomes as hard as fired brick and quite unamenable to either cultivation or colonization by wild plants. Laterite is the prime natural roadmaking material in the tropics; the laterite blocks from which the temples of Angkor in Cambodia were built have withstood the onslaughts of weather and war for nearly two thousand years. Tropical forests grow on lateritic soils only because of the ultrarapid nutrient cycling and only while the canopy provides a continuous shield from the direct heat of the sun.

The temperate rain forests of the western United States grow on podzol soils, which are acidic because of the high carbon-dioxide-rich rainfall and the decomposition of acid-producing coniferous leaf needles. However, whereas in a tropical setting the humus layer would be no more than a few centimeters thick and poor in nutrients, the lower year-round temperate temperatures, which fall below freezing in winter, allow the accumulation of humus to a thickness that may exceed twelve inches (30 cm) and provide a rich supply of nutrients. The absolute growth rate of temperate rain-forest trees is probably faster than their tropical counterparts and discounting the six months of dormancy during the northern winter, the growth rate becomes almost twice as fast. When one considers that the light levels are much lower than in the tropics, it can be determined that the temperate trees are much more efficient. This superiority in performance probably depends on the supply of nutrients, for without the raw materials for making new cells, energy alone is inadequate.

The chronic shortage of nutrients in rain-forest soils has led to the development of a number of special features that seem related to enhancing the supply of nutrients. For

Left. *The full glory of the tropical streams is only to be found in waterfalls such as this one at La Selva in Costa Rica. The splash and spray ensure a luxuriant growth of mosses, liverworts, and other water-loving plants on the rock face.*

Above. (left) *The seeds of epiphytes do not choose their germination sites. Presumably, a bird either wiped its beak or defecated on this Trinidadian telephone line and the seed of* Tillandsia bulbosa *(Bromeliaceae) germinated* in situ.

(right) *The geology of the bedrock may not affect the species composition of the vegetation that grows on the surface, but it has a profound effect on the detailed topography. This waterfall at Ramboda in Sri Lanka has cut through a series of alternating horizontal hard and soft rocks, producing a staircase over which the water falls.*

Right. (top) *This fern* (Dipteris conjugata) *extends its solar-panel leaf to intercept the insolation of the sun. Chlorophyll, the green pigment of land-plant tissue, is the life-blood of plants, for without it they would be unable to harness the energy of sunlight for growth and repair. Surplus energy is carried from the leaves to other needy parts of the plant in the form of atomic bonds in sugar molecules.*

(bottom) *Reminiscent of the feather of a giant bird, the delicate foliage of a tree fern* (Cyathea) *wafts gently in the forest breeze. Why the fronds of these ferns are so finely divided is obscure. Perhaps it is to ensure good air circulation over the surface, for only by the evaporation of water at the leaf surface can nutrients be drawn in through the roots in adequate amounts.*

example, many of the larger tropical trees become hollow in the center as they age. Whether this condition is a handicap or an advantage to the tree is a current topic of debate. The advocates for it being an advantage argue that the old heartwood is no loss to the tree, as it only represents a past dumping site for waste material. By allowing fungi and bacteria to penetrate the bark and provide a means of access for insects and other excavators, the hollow trunk ultimately becomes a roosting site for birds, bats, and other animals. Donald Perry has taken inventories of the animals inhabiting hollow trees and has found extraordinarily complex communities residing in the trunks and hollow roots. Feces, urine, and feeding wastes fall to the bottom of the core and, ideally, provide a source of nutrients available only to the tree which is providing the shelter. By making the decomposition products of its own core available to itself, the tree can, theoretically at least, convert a large trunk that is a solid rod into one that is a hollow cylinder. From an engineering standpoint, such a change is desirable, for a hollow cylinder is more resistant to bending than a solid rod of similar weight.

The antagonists of this view of the function of hollow trunks claim the obvious truth that no advantage has been demonstrated experimentally, and that once the decomposition of the core has begun, the tree has no way of controlling it. The tree, therefore, has sown the seed of its own destruction. Furthermore, the antagonists are quick to point out that epiphytes frequently trail their roots into the hollow cores and share in the nutritional bonanza.

Incidentally, it seems possible that buttress roots also serve as traps for forest litter, for litter accumulates between them to levels that are uncommon elsewhere on the forest floor. These pockets of detritus serve as retreats for small terrestrial animals and thus may add to the nutrients that are available to the tree. Stilt and prop roots may also serve as traps for litter and silt in times of flood and thus improve the fertility of the soil around the plant.

The nutrients absorbed by the root systems of forest plants are essentially similar in all species; thus the substances released by the decomposition of the litter layer are also rather uniform. It is for this reason that the forests which grow on tropical soils only occasionally reflect the underlying differences in soil type. Fred Hardy, Professor Emeritus of the Imperial College of Tropical Agriculture in Trinidad, has demonstrated that soil and vegetation surveys there show little correlation. In effect, the forest makes its own topsoil regardless of the nature of the parent rock from which the underlying subsoil is derived. It is impossible to guess the agricultural value of tropical land by looking at the undisturbed natural vegetation.

Between 10 and 15 percent of all known tropical soils are derived from old sandy beaches and are known as white sands. These coarse-grained quartzite soils are highly porous, poor in nutrients, and occur in many lowland tropical river basins. They are well known in South America, Africa, Malaya, and the Indonesian islands. Daniel Janzen, of the University of Pennsylvania, has proposed a unifying theory to account for the exceptionally poor land and aquatic fauna associated with these soils.

Janzen's argument is that because these white sands are so weak in the retention of minerals, the plants that grow on them have to protect themselves to an exceptional degree against nutrient loss. The loss of a leaf to a caterpillar or other herbivore is a loss of material that cannot easily be replaced, hence the plants protect themselves against herbivore damage by depositing poisons in their tissues. Protection by dependence on toxic compounds has been highly successful in some of these forests and they support so few insects that the bird population is severely depressed. Early travelers found the silence of these forests so uncanny that they spawned legends of lost worlds and other myths. It is not surprising to find that the families of plants which inhabit white sands are already well known for their poisonous properties. Because there are relatively few species that can withstand the rigors of these hostile habitats, the species diversity is much reduced when compared with nearby forests on richer soils.

The key issue is that the fallen leaves and other plant parts are so well protected with poisons that they take a long time to decompose, keeping their nutrients out of circulation for that period. The energy they contain can no longer be applied toward building litter organisms and so the soil fauna is meager. Furthermore, the detoxification of

Above. *The brilliant contrasts of sunlight and darkness add excitement to tropical storms. The elegant highlights here are in the rain forest at Ratnapura in Sri Lanka. The noise of the torrential rain is deafening and can be heard from well over a mile away.*

Opposite. (top) *Tropical storms are humiliating, for even within the security of one's home, the onslaught of nature reminds us that we are human, frail, and at the mercy of the elements. Only at sea is the emotion more overwhelming.*

(bottom) *The forest at Rancho Grande in Venezuela was one of William Beebe's early research sites. It was in the litter under this forest that he first emphasized the richness, diversity, and importance of the tropical soil fauna.*

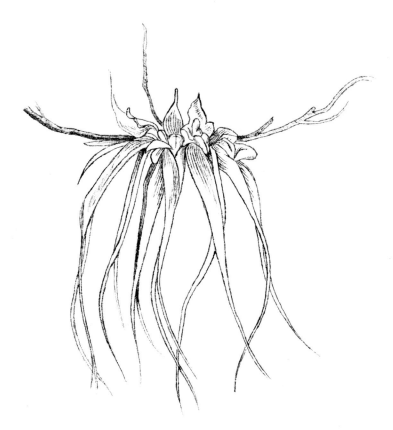

the phenolic compounds in the leaves produces humic acids that render the soils extremely acid (pH 3 to 4), a factor that further weakens the power of the soil to hold nutrients against the heavy rains. In the white sand forests of Sarawak, the only vertebrates Janzen found were lizards in the litter layer and other mobile animals that could forage elsewhere.

A related effect is that the toxic compounds from the litter layer are washed into streams and rivers and effectively poison them. The phenolic compounds turn the water a clear brown, which when viewed from above appears black without seeming muddy. These blackwater rivers have been known for centuries, as the abundance of South American rivers named Río Negro testifies. These blackwater rivers are notoriously, and gratefully, free of those biting insects which have aquatic larvae, but unfortunately they are also almost devoid of fishes. The fishes that do occur are mostly surface feeders or partial air breathers.

When Daniel Janzen first proposed his explanation of the poor productivity of white sand soils and blackwater rivers, his hypothesis was greeted with overt skepticism by some tropical botanists. Just recently, Doyle McKey and his associates have demonstrated that the phenolic compounds in the leaves of vegetation on a white sand site in the Cameroons were twice as high as those on a more fertile lateritic site in Uganda. Janzen's hypothesis is on its way to becoming a theory.

The vegetative changes that take place naturally during the colonization of bare earth first by lichens and mosses, then by weedy annuals and woody plants, and ultimately by the mature forest, are known as primary succession. Recently erupted volcanoes offer unique opportunities for the study of such succession but require a long-term investment of time, effort, and money, all of which are in short supply to the modern scientist. One of the better-studied examples of primary succession leading to tropical rain forest is that conducted on the volcanic island of Krakatoa, between Java and Sumatra, which erupted in 1883 and became a desert in 1884. By the 1950s it was clothed with a substantial covering of rain forest.

The underlying principles of succession are that the early pioneer plants change the environment by supplying shade and moisture-retaining organic matter to the soil. Thus, the pioneers provide conditions in which new species of plants can grow that would have been unable to survive on naked soil. In turn, these plants are succeeded by other species that are favored by further changes in the environment. The floristic change that takes place when existing vegetation is cut or otherwise disturbed is known as secondary succession and the immediately resultant vegetation is termed "secondary growth." This term contrasts with the term "primary growth" or "virgin forest," which is meant to imply that the vegetation has never been disturbed and is mature, as the result of infinite years of succession.

There are few primary rain forests left in the world other than in parts of the Congo and Amazon basins. Ecologists term the mature forest "climax" forest, insinuating that it has reached an ultimate stability in species composition. Whether the primary rain forests still remaining are truly climax formations is a matter of dispute, for there are many unexplained anomalies.

In the rain forests that have become damaged by natural catastrophe or by human activity, great changes take place. Whereas in undisturbed forest the only seedlings that can germinate are those of the existing forest trees and those adapted to growing in the weak light of the forest floor, the cleared forest is invaded by plants that are colonizers of more open ground and require a high level of light intensity. The rapid exploitation of such opportunities by so-called weedy species leads to the rapid growth of secondary forest, which has a very different species composition from that of the preceding primary forest. The rapidly growing *Cecropia* in America, *Musanga* in Africa, and *Macaranga* in Malaya are short-lived, even though they may exceed sixty feet (18 m) in height, and are soon replaced by slower-growing species.

As the secondary forest develops, it becomes a haven for vines that are insufficiently woody to attain great height and so becomes an impenetrable "jungle." Only when the lower level of the canopy has attained a height of about forty feet (12 m) will the forest take on some of the characteristics of the mature tropical rain forest. Partly because of the different species composition but largely because the vegetation is nearer the ground, the fauna of the secondary forest differs markedly from that of the mature forest. Most popular zoo animals, such as monkeys, apes, and leopards, are characteristic inhabitants of the secondary forest.

A detailed examination of many apparently mature tropical rain forests presents a paradoxical situation, for the composition of the sapling flora does not match that of the overshadowing canopy. Some tree species seem superabundant, whereas others are not represented at all. Presumably, the growing conditions are suitable for plants while they are saplings, but do not suit them when they are mature, a situation that is incompatible with the stability of climax vegetation. Data from Puerto Rico over a thirty-year period show that substantial portions of the rain forest are damaged by hurricanes at intervals of about ten years. Under these frequencies the expectation of finding undisturbed tropical rain forest is small, for all over the tropical world high winds, in the form of tornadoes and hurricanes in the Americas and cyclones and typhoons in the Far East, are commonplace. It would seem that most, if not all, tropical forests are in the process of recovery from disturbance by the natural catastrophes of fire, wind, or flood. Genuine climax formations are perhaps an elusive and unattainable goal. The tragedy is that even if we were to undertake long-range studies to elucidate the complex driving forces of the tropical rain forest, the forests will have been destroyed by commercial development long before any valuable data could have been gathered.

Following pages. This tree at six thousand feet (1,800 m) in Costa Rica shows the density of epiphytic ferns, orchids, lichens, and bromeliads that can maintain themselves on a tree limb. Isolated trees, or trees at the forest margins, are usually the most heavily colonized, for the limbs are more uniformly illuminated than those of the forest interior.

Squatters in the Sky

The foliage of a tree is its lifeline to the sun. Collectively, the canopy of the forest is a massive solar panel, absorbing light and using it to build energy-rich substances which can be moved to other sites within the trees. The "power cells" of the foliage are the richest food resource for forest herbivores, so it is logical that we should find that the majority of the larger animals of the tropical rain forest live within the canopy. Insects, lizards, frogs, birds, bats, and other mammals inhabit the canopy and are rarely seen by travelers on the forest floor.

It is not only animals that exploit the canopy layers, for small plants from the microscopic to the ponderous have also made their homes in the treetops. The algae, lichens, and liverworts that adhere to the surfaces of thick, durable leaves are known as epiphyllae, and can pirate light from the entire leaf surface. The limitations of the area of the available surface and the strength of the leaf's attachment prevent these encrusting organisms from attaining large size, but similar species growing on the bark of branches can cover large areas. Competition for space is keen, so the more minute organisms are usually confined to the smaller, more delicate surfaces that cannot be colonized by the larger plants. The lateral branches, crotches, and rougher tree bark carry a comprehensive burden of mosses, ferns, and flowering plants of such families as Bromeliaceae and Orchidaceae. These plants which grow on tree trunks and branches and have no root connection with the soil are termed "epiphytes."

Amateur and professional horticulturists are familiar with epiphytes, for many of the most beautiful of the cultivated orchids are epiphytic and are displayed in hanging baskets or on pieces of tree-fern trunk. Orchid fanciers have now developed cloning techniques that enable a single plant to become the parent of thousands of exact genetic copies. Such cloned seedlings are now available at the larger flower shows in the United States and Europe. Bromeliads are also strong favorites, for their splendid floral and leaf colors make a spectacular display.

Garden-shop customers should be aware that many bromeliads flower only once, so the bloom you see when you purchase the plant may be the only one! However, if the plant is in good health new flowers will arise from lateral shoots. Pitcher plants, also popular, are not epiphytes but are climbers rooted in the soil. All these plants will be discussed in this chapter together with some epiphytes which have less visual impact but which have developed a fascinating relationship with ants.

Most epiphytes depend on their host only for support and do little damage other than hold moisture and, perhaps, facilitate the entry of pathogenic bacteria and fungi. However, during torrential rain the addition of water to an already heavy burden of epiphytes may cause the breaking of a limb. Solitary trees, isolated in their youth, are most often damaged in this way because their branching is more extensive and the leverage applied in the spreading canopy may become more than the tree can bear.

As trees age, the bark becomes rougher and more amenable to colonization by epiphytes. The smooth bark of young tropical rain-forest trees may be an adaptation to avoid heavy epiphytic infestations. Bamboos, for example, with their ultrasmooth bark, rarely support any epiphytes larger than lichens. Little is known about the capacity of tree bark to secrete antiepiphyte compounds but such may well exist, for the epiphytic burden of mangroves is always meager and may be related to high levels of tannin in the bark.

Although the distribution of epiphytes depends on the branching habit of the tree and the physical and chemical characteristics of the bark, there are zones within the canopy that favor certain epiphytes. The lowest (C) level is cooler, less windy, darker, and more constant than the A and B levels above. It is in this lower level that the greatest number of shade-loving epiphytes, such as mosses, ferns, and some orchids, are found. In the crown centers of the higher levels, the epiphytes are sun-loving but are without specialized water-conserving features. Only the most drought-resistant plants, such as the bromeliads and some orchids, can endure the desiccation from the fierce heat and wind of the highest levels. Some botanists feel that the drought-resistant adaptations of these epiphytes indicate that they may have their historical roots in the arid climates of temperate regions.

The hazards of being an epiphyte revolve around remaining in position, acquiring nutrients, and resisting periodic droughts, for sunlight and atmospheric carbon dioxide are available in abundance. Their rooting systems are principally holdfasts for binding tightly to the bark of the trunk or limb, although small quantities of nutrients may be extracted from bark by some epiphytic species.

The root tissue of many epiphytes has an outer layer of dead cells which absorb moisture from the atmosphere when it is humid, but which contract to form a waterproof covering when they are dry. Specialized cells below the dead layer pass any absorbed water to conducting cells, which take it to other parts of the plant. Other epiphytes have equally specialized methods of reducing water loss. In some species the stomal leaf pores are guarded by clusters of humidity-sensitive hairs that contract over the pore and partially close it when it is dry, but stand erect and leave the pathway clear when it is humid. Other species close their pores during the heat of the day and open them only at night. Normally this rhythm would inhibit the synthesis of sugars by limiting the supply of atmospheric carbon dioxide, but the plant stores the carbon dioxide it has taken in during the night, when the pores were open, for use during the day.

The epiphytic Bromeliaceae are known in Trinidad as "wild pines" because of their similarity to the foliage of the commercial pineapple. Elsewhere they are usually referred to as "tank epiphytes" because of their water-holding capacity. The bases of their long, narrow leaves bind tightly around the stem in the shape of a conical funnel and can

Right. *Plants that grow on the leaves of other plants are known as epiphyllae. In this example from Kinabalu rain forest, a stellate lichen is growing on the surface of a tree leaf. Notice the typical rain-forest leaf shape with a smooth margin and a pointed drip tip, which aids in shedding water.*

Center. *This leaf from Manaus, Brazil, is encrusted with epiphyllic liverworts. Dense growth of epiphyllae can shield the leaf from sunlight and seriously reduce its photosynthetic activity. The leaf can become a liability to the parent plant rather than an asset.*

Bottom. *Plants that grow on the twigs, branches, or trunks of trees, but not on the leaves, are known as epiphytes. This tree from Mount Kinabalu is overgrown with epiphytes, including the orchid* Dendrochilum. *Isolated trees can become so heavily infested with epiphytes that their branches break off from an additional load of heavy rain.*

Above. *Bromeliaceae, which are characteristic of tropical America, frequently have all-red flowers or cream-colored flowers surrounded by large bright red bracts—as in this* Guzmania lingulata *from Ecuador. Most bromeliads are pollinated by hummingbirds or bats.*

Left. *This unusual lichen,* Teloschistes exilis, *from Amazonian Brazil, resembles a cluster of amphibian eggs. More ordinary lichens are above and below the central mass. Lichens are all associations of a fungus and an alga; the two organisms sometimes seem unable to exist without the presence of the other. The relationship is mutually beneficial, for the alga synthesizes sugar by photosynthesis while the fungus provides a moist, secure habitat and extracts nutrients from the environment.*

hold up to two gallons (5 l). *Tillandsia bulbosa* has its leaves meeting over the top of its "tank" and can be inverted without loss of water. Tank bromeliads attain remarkable size, for in Trinidad *Glomeropitcairnia erectifolia* can reach nine feet tall (2.7 m). Excess water in epiphytes is most commonly stored in fleshy leaves, but the Orchidaceae contains many species in which water is stored in bulbous bases to the stems. The retention of water enables the plant to grow continuously even during conditions of drought.

Perhaps the most critical factor in the growth of epiphytes is the supply of nitrogen. Some epiphyllic blue-green algae, and those lichens with the appropriate algal—fungal association, are able to synthesize soluble nitrate from atmospheric nitrogen, but for the remainder of the epiphytes the only source is from detritus within reach of the roots and perhaps dissolved in rain during thunderstorms. Only those epiphytes which are relatively low in the forest canopy are favored by fruit, seeds, leaf litter, animal feces, and feeding waste falling down from above. Epiphytic rooting systems usually form a bird's-nest-like network, which is effective in trapping detritus. The leaves may also assist in trapping litter by forming a cup against the bark of the tree. The winds that blow across the forest canopy will bring some organic dust, although the extent of such additional nutrients is important only at the margins of the forest. The ensheathing root systems of epiphytes provide good nesting sites for ants, and these insects are, perhaps, the most beneficial source of nitrogen, for their feces, feeding waste, and nest-building materials all contain valuable nutrients.

Some epiphytes, which grow in especially nutrient-poor situations, have developed intimate and specific relationships with ants. The first of two types of ant/epiphyte interaction is illustrated by Janzen's descriptions of a remarkable association between the epiphytes *Hydnophytum formicarium, Myrmecodia tuberosa, Phymatodes sinuosa,* and *Dischidia rafflesiana* and the unaggressive ant *Iridomyrmex myrmecodiae* from the white sands of Sarawak. The situation is exemplified by that of *H. formicarium* (Rubiaceae), which has a swollen stem base, perhaps for use as a storage organ for starch, and is replete with a labyrinth of tunnel-like cavities. The tunnels are not made by the ants, but are natural and have a few large circular exit holes on the side of the tuberous stem where it abuts the host tree. In addition, there are many small holes that serve to ventilate the gas exchange between the tuber and the surrounding air. The ants colonize the interior cavities, and where the tunnel walls are dry, smooth, and nonabsorbent they keep their brood. Where the tunnels end blindly the walls are rough and absorbent, and these areas serve as dumps for the ants' feeding waste.

Janzen assumes that the epiphyte absorbs nutrients from these garbage heaps. The absence of fungal growth suggests that the plant may produce a fungicide to keep the cavities clean. A second benefit from the ant relationship is that the ants cement the epiphyte to the substrate tree by packing the interface of the epiphyte and the substrate with earth mâché, prepared by masticating plant material and soil. As this mâché covers the roots of the epiphyte, it may be an additional source of nutrients. Another astonishing feature of the relationship is that although the fruits of the epiphyte are eaten by birds, the ants collect the ripe seeds and sow them in the earth material around the roots. If the epiphyte should be dislodged by a storm or by becoming too heavy, it is likely to be replaced by a plant from one of its own seeds. Janzen counted 12,640 worker ants and 46 winged reproductive in a single tuber.

A second and rather different example of epiphytic specialization is seen in *Dischidia rafflesiana* (Asclepiadaceae), in which some leaves are modified to form a hollow receptacle with an aperture near the junction of blade and leaf stalk. Again it is *I. myromecodiae* which invades the cavity and uses the chamber to raise its brood. After the brood has matured, the ants begin to pack the cavity with the remains of insects and other small animals until ultimately the chamber is filled with animal debris. As soon as the animal fragments are added to the chamber, plant rootlets which had up to that time remained small begin to enlarge and invade the chamber. Presumably, the plant gains a source of nutrients from the decomposing material wrapped up in its leaves.

These particular observations were made in Sarawak, but these ant-plants are known throughout Southeast Asia from Malaya to northern Australia and the Pacific islands. In each case the ant involved seems to be the same species. That these ant-plant relationships are beneficial can be inferred from the density of these epiphytes in a single locality surveyed by Janzen. He found in a single plot 30 feet by 82 feet (9 m by 25 m): 494 *Hydnophytum*, 31 *Myrmecodia*, 20 *Dischidia*, 2 *Phymatodes*, in addition to 41 *Pachycentrum* and 72 miscellaneous orchids. The benefit for the ant is housing with a humid atmosphere. The plant obtains nitrogen and perhaps raised levels of carbon dioxide from the respiration of the ants.

The competition for nitrogen is so keen that some plants which begin their lives as epiphytes and so gain a toehold in the canopy then develop pendulous roots that are extended downward until they reach the ground. Once in the soil, an enhanced supply of nutrients and water enables the plant to grow rapidly and even overtake the whole canopy of the supporting tree. Most prominent in African and Southeast Asian rain forests are the strangler figs, which germinate from seeds lodged in the crotch of a tree and send down several aerial roots to ground level. Once rooted, the roots and stems proliferate and surround the trunk of the supporting tree, while the foliage of the fig grows rapidly and shades out the canopy. Eventually, the host tree dies and leaves the dead trunk surrounded tightly by the scaffolding of the fig. Strangler figs may overtake abandoned buildings in the same way.

Every possible growth pattern is to be found in the tropical rain forest. While epiphytes send down their

Following pages. (left) *Encrusting lichens, such as* Herpothallon sanguineum *from Amazonas, Brazil, display superb colors. The specific name of this lichen, meaning bloodlike, clearly refers to the decorated margin. No function is known for these pigments.*

(top left) *The roots of epiphytes do not obtain water or nutrients from the plants on which they grow. They are not parasites. Epiphytes extract water from the humid atmosphere with special cells and they absorb nutrients from organic matter that accumulates around their roots. These roots are of* Philodendron *(Araceae) from Sri Lanka.*

(top right) *This epiphytic climbing fern* (Trichomanes tuerckheimii) *from Manaus, Brazil, could hardly get any closer to its support.*

(bottom) *The water trapped within the closely overlapping bracts creates interference rings that resemble the ripples on a pond. The plant is the cup-of-flame bromeliad* (Neoregalia carolinae) *from Brazil.*

trailing roots, vines send up their clinging stems which germinate from seeds on the forest floor. The vines of the mature forest are shade tolerant in their youth but eventually envelop the highest levels of the canopy and enjoy the full light of the sun. The greatest growth of vines is found in light gaps and on the edges of the forest, where they are chiefly responsible for the wall of solid green that one sees from the river. In temperate forests, the herbaceous, nonwoody climbing vines die back each winter, but in the tropical rain forest the continuously favorable growing conditions allow climbers to become long-lived and develop thick, woody stems. These perennial climbers are properly termed "lianas."

In Southeast Asia, climbing palms are a characteristic feature of the vegetation and although most are less than 200 feet long (60 m) some specimens have been measured at more than 785 feet (240 m). Of course, not all of this length was directed upward! Lianas can pose challenging puzzles, for sometimes their lowest contact with their substrate tree is a great height from the ground. Explanations for these situations include the unsound assumption that the substrate and the liana have grown up together since their youth, or that the original support has now decayed. Although heavy growth of lianas can break off branches or cause crowns to become so misshapen that the balance of the tree is seriously disturbed, the most common effect is to shade out the foliage of the tree and ultimately kill it. Lianas are a conspicuous feature of forests with the substantial tree crown damage that is produced by hurricanes.

A special type of vine was discovered in 1658 by E. de Flacourt in Madagascar but the botanical description of *Nepenthes* did not follow until 1797. The Nepenthaceae, or pitcher-plant vines, are characterized by the modifications to some of the leaves to form a liquid-containing pitcher, complete with lid. Secretions of nectar on the lower surface of the open lid and around the rim of the pitcher attract a variety of insects, especially ants and flies. The insect visitors frequently lose their grip on the waxy or slick sides of the pitcher and fall into the liquid at the bottom. Downward-pointing hairs on the waxy sides of the vessel prevent their escape. Digestive enzymes secreted by the sides of the pitcher, and aided by bacteria in the liquid, rapidly decompose the body of the victim and render its nutrients available to the plant. The discovery of rodent teeth inside a large *Nepenthes* has spawned tales of mammal-trapping pitcher plants, but although an occasional squirrel or tree rat has undoubtedly been caught, such events are rare. The Nepenthaceae are now well known in the higher-altitude rain forests of Southeast Asia, Indonesia, Sri Lanka, Madagascar, the York Peninsula of Australia, the Khasi highlands of northern India, and southern China.

Carnivorous plants, such as the so-called pitcher plants of other families in the temperate rain forests of the United States, and such novelties as Venus's fly-traps and sundews are all characteristic of plants living in nitrogen-deficient habitats. Horticulturists who overfertilize their pitcher

plants discover that the characteristic pitchers do not develop.

However, the pitcher plant is not always 100 percent successful, for some mosquitoes "helicopter" down into the pitcher and lay their egg rafts on the surface of the liquid. When the eggs hatch, the larvae seem immune to digestion and share the future victims with the plant. Similarly, some flesh flies give birth to living larvae on the lid of the pitcher, from whence they wriggle into the liquid and continue their development. When mature, they bore a hole in the side of the pitcher and fall to the ground to pupate. The spiders *Thomisus nepenthiphilus* and *Misumenops nepenthicola* weave their webs over the walls of the pitcher and intercept victims on their way down!

Although the watery fluid inside the pitcher is alleged to cure a multitude of human ailments, the only confirmed effect is to produce constipation. Travelers often use the pitchers of the larger species as water jugs, for they can hold more than half a gallon. Potable water can be obtained from young unopened pitchers or, if available, from the hollow stems of the larger bamboos.

Many animals have taken advantage of the favorable microhabitats supplied by epiphytes. Frogs and dragonflies may pass their whole developmental life in the waters of tank bromeliads. The epiphytes are a rich botanical and zoological garden squatting in the forest canopy, stealing light and nutrients from their hosts.

Opposite. *The epiphytic orchid* Epidendrum difforme *is only one of many types of plants growing on this tree trunk. Notice the orchid stems swollen with water toward the bottom of the picture. These structures are known as pseudobulbs. The broad fingerlike leaves toward the top of the picture are those of a tank bromeliad.*

Above. *The Brazilian orchid* Isabella virginalis *has its pseudobulbs ensheathed in tissue with resistant fibers, so that when the intervening tissue has rotted away, the fibrous network remains, perhaps to collect nourishing organic matter such as animal feces and displaced plant material falling from above.*

Following pages. *The trunk and spines of this red silk-cotton* (Bombax malabaricum) *from Indochina are veritable botanic gardens, replete with encrusting and foliaceous lichens, mosses, and fungi.*

Left. *Roots sent down by arboreal epiphytes in Sumatra give a Tarzanian aspect to the forest. Water usually limits the growth of true epiphytes, but once contact with the ground is made by these aerial roots the growth rate increases markedly. The roots themselves are extremely strong and can carry a great weight—it is the attachment of the epiphyte to the tree that makes swinging on them hazardous.*

Above. (left) *Coarse bark is not confined to large trees. The strangler fig (*Ficus sp.*) that is constricting the smooth-barked host has a deeply fissured bark even though it is no more than three inches (7.5 cm) in diameter. Notice how the trunk of the host has already become twisted by the forces exerted by the fig.*

(right) *The rootlike structures enveloping this mature tree also belong to the strangler fig. The fig germinates as an epiphyte and lowers roots to the ground. As soon as rooting in the ground has been established, the epiphyte grows rapidly, both upward and downward, and eventually completely encircles the host tree, which usually dies from having its own foliage smothered by that of the fig.*

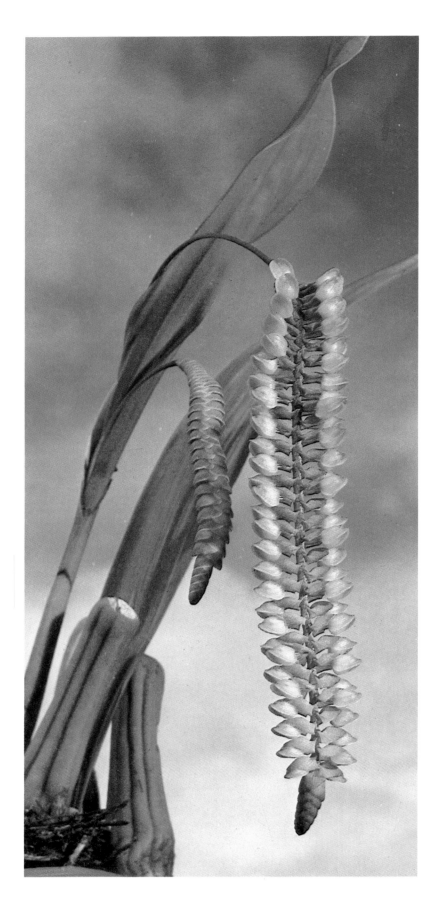

Opposite. (left) *There can be few more suitable common names than that of the "rattlesnake orchid." The epiphytic* Pholidota imbricata *can be found from India to the Philippines.*

(right) *The bark of this tree* (Cinnamomum ovalifolium) *is used as a cinnamon substitute. The abundance of lichens would not impair the value of the bark for this use, for the lichens use the bark only as an attachment substrate, not as a source of nutrients. Lichens are very sensitive to air pollution and different species are used as an early warning system for pollution levels in North America.*

Left. (top) *This species of* Tillandsia *from Brazil demonstrates the additional lure to pollinators supplied by the leaves. The flowers are relatively inconspicuous, but the weak floral display is amplified by stunning red foliage.*

(bottom) *Nitrogen for the synthesis of proteins and nucleic acids is critical in the lives of many plants, and one method of supplementing nitrogen is to trap insects. The Nepenthaceae, or pitcher plants, all use modified leaves as traps baited with sweet- or foul-smelling attractants. Insects settle on the rim of the pitcher, slip on the slick sides, and fall into the pitcher. In the bottom of the pitcher is liquid which contains digestive enzymes. The undigestible remains of the victims accumulate in the pitcher as testimony to their contribution to the life of the plant.* Nepenthes villosa *is illustrated from Mount Kinabalu. Notice the lid which deflects rain away from the mouth of the pitcher.*

Animals of the Forest Floor

The popular concept of tropical jungle has elephants, rhinoceroses, lions, and leopards rampaging through the undergrowth while giant serpents leer down from overhanging branches, poised ready to swallow up the unwary traveler. Romantic and exciting? Perhaps. But factually correct? No. The truth is that the forest interior is poorly supplied with large ground-dwelling animals for the simple reason that there is very little for them to eat.

The foliage of most rain-forest trees is so high that it is not within reach of animals that browse, and there are no grasses on which to graze. The food resources of animals are restricted to soil fungi, the sparse ground flora and fruits, and dead plant material that has fallen from the canopy. As would be expected, the largest populations of animals on the forest floor are those that feed on microorganisms living in the soil.

To give some credence to these statements, one only has to look at the data generated by one of the few careful investigations that have been made of tropical rain-forest fauna. In 1973, E. J. Fittkau and H. Klinge of the Max-Planck Institute of Western Germany published their report of a thorough study of an area near Manaus in the heart of the Amazonian rain forest. The site chosen was one that was not seasonally flooded, for flood-free terra firma localities are faunistically richer than those of the várzea, where the organisms have to withstand the hazards of annual inundation. The sample area was carefully and systematically felled. Every plant and animal was identified as far as was possible, counted, and weighed. Large trees, including the roots, were cut up, weighed, and their remains transported to Europe for dry-weight and mineral analysis. The plant counts show that the flora was rich, for on an area of about two and one-half acres (1 ha) they found 93,780 trees over 100 feet tall (38 m). The total weight of the living plant material was 925 tons, of which 2 percent was leaves, 50 percent was stems and trunks, 21 percent was branches and twigs, and 27 percent was roots. The dead plant material lying on the ground weighed 58 tons, so added together the living and dead plant material weighed 983 tons. Against this massive weight of wood and leaves, the animals weighed only one quarter of a ton and half of them lived in the top four inches (10 cm) of soil. Thus, in a vertical section of a forest over 100 feet tall, 50 percent of the animals live in less than 0.5 percent of the height at the surface of the soil! Why?

The chief reason for the depauperized fauna of the tropical rain forests seems to be that with year-round breeding potential, the hazards to plants of attack by herbivorous insects and mammals is so great that nearly all plants protect themselves with poisonous compounds in their leaves and wood. Only after branches, twigs, leaves, and other detritus fall to the ground and die can fungi and bacteria break them into compounds that can be assimilated by other organisms. However, when the fungi have consumed it, the food material is in ultrasmall packages only harvestable by minute organisms, hence the abundance of microscopic animals, most of which probably feed directly on the fungi themselves. This situation is again reflected in the kinds of animals found by L. Beck in a comparable area nearby. In two and a half acres of forest floor, Beck calculated that there were 727 million mites, 120 million springtail insects, and 40 million scale insects and aphids. His figure of 8.6 million ants is probably low, for ants have a clumped distribution centered on their nests. These figures are not exceptional, for comparable data from other localities show that in a monsoon rain forest in Puerto Rico the weight of terrestrial animals comprised only 0.1 percent of the total living material and 0.02 percent in another study in central Amazonia.

The popular imagination associates spectacular plants with spectacular animals, but not even the meanest, leanest tiger could make a living in the rain forest studied by Fittkau and Klinge! For the animals that hunt on the ground, it is not the impoverished tropical rain forest that provides the good life but the savannas and grasslands. These ecosystems are the most productive in the tropics and are where most of the large cats live. Populations of hoofed game animals frequently have been recorded in East Africa at levels of one-third of a ton per two and a half acres (300 kg per ha). The grass supports the game and the game supports the large predators. On all tropical rain-forest floors the composition of the fauna of the litter layer is basically similar and consists of small insects, mites, pseudoscorpions, millipedes, and an occasional lizard or frog. Only an expert in the identification of a particular group of animals could tell whether rain-forest soil came from Africa, America, or Malaya.

The microorganisms that decompose the organic matter in the surface soil are aided by bacteria and single-celled animals in the alimentary canals of termites, cockroaches, and beetles. It is remarkable that even though the insects have a history spanning nearly 400 million years, only a few species of timber-boring beetle larvae have acquired the ability to digest cellulose, the chief ingredient in the walls of plant cells. The ubiquitous termites depend on protozoa, which permanently inhabit their gut, for cellulose digestion, and similarly the ants that cultivate fungus gardens use the fungi to digest the cellulose of their plant harvests, for they themselves are unable to do it alone.

These cooperative relationships between insects and their microorganism guests are efficient, for at the warm temperatures and humidities of the forest floor only the largest tree trunks persist for much longer than a year; the smaller twigs and branches are recycled within a few weeks. The decomposition of fallen wood would be even faster if it were not for compounds deposited by the tree to protect the living tissues from attack by pathogenic organisms. A substantial amount of the energy budgets of living trees is devoted to these secondary compounds, which in extreme cases render wood almost totally resistant to insect attack or decay. John D. Bultman and Charles R. Southwell of the United States Naval Research Laboratory have spent more

Opposite. (top left) *Tree frogs are famous for their cryptic camouflage. Even an experienced herpetologist could be forgiven for walking by this* Hyla pardalis *from Brazil, for on a lichen-covered tree trunk it is almost invisible. Notice the expanded tips to the fingers with which it maintains its grip on a vertical surface.*

(top right) *Edible frogs are usually cryptically colored, but many tropical frogs are extremely poisonous and are usually brightly colored. This Brazilian* Phyllobates *has typical black-and-yellow warning coloration and is avoided by all but the most naive predators. Some American Indians tip their spears and darts in the poison from these frogs.*

(bottom) *The gliding gecko* (Ptychozoon kuhli) *of the Southeast Asian rain forests is a famous lizard with flaplike folds of skin between the fingers, toes, arms, legs, and tail. It escapes predators by leaping into space with all its flaps of skin extended and clutching the first object it strikes.*

Above. *This Colombian* Hyla labialis *(Hylidae) shows the typical tree-frog appearance. The fingers and toes have adhesive pads for gripping the slick, waxy leaf surfaces and enable them to climb glass in captivity. A few species of tree frog have managed to overcome the need to depend on water for the development of their young. They lay eggs in protective nests of leaves in the tree canopy and endow them with sufficient yolk to carry the embryo through the tadpole stage to emerge as a miniature adult.*

than twenty years investigating the resistance of tropical woods to attack by insects and microorganisms. Wood is a popular material for the construction of pier pilings, docks, warehouses, and other buildings in the tropics, and resistance to attack is an important economic factor in the choice of tree species. As is so often the case, the best woods are from slow-growing tropical trees that are far from common. Those favorable species which were known to occur in dense stands were cut down long ago.

The abundance of nutrients in dead vegetation falling from the forest canopy is rather meager, for the trees withdraw all readily salvageable nutrients from a leaf before it is severed from its parent twig. Dead branches are usually honeycombed with borer tunnels long before they break off. Only fruits and seeds have a substantial nutritional investment. The poor foundation of nutrients on the forest floor cannot support a large mass of consumers, hence the animal food chains are short.

Mites, springtails, and millipedes feed on the soil fungi and are preyed on by pseudoscorpions, centipedes, and small insects, which in turn are eaten by spiders, scorpions, lizards, frogs, small snakes, turtles, and insectivorous mammals. The larger insectivores are eaten by carnivorous reptiles, birds, and mammals. At each level of consumption, the amount of weight retained is only about one tenth of the weight of food eaten, so it is clear that the weight, or biomass, of the higher-level predators must be much less than that of the animals lower down the chain. Although the 10-percent conversion rate is subject to numerous exceptions, it is a useful generalization and in common terms means that it takes 100 pounds of grass to make 10 pounds of cow, and it takes 10 pounds of cow to make 1 pound of human.

The vertebrates that are first in the feeding line, or in ecological terms "on the lowest trophic level," are the litter-inhabiting frogs and lizards. Again, the American rain forests have the richest fauna. Norman J. Scott, of the Biological Sciences Group of the University of Connecticut, has shown that the vertebrate abundance in the litter layer of Costa Rican rain forests is ten times larger than that of similar forests in Borneo. Presumably this is because the rate of litter fall is greater. Over a two-and-a-half-acre plot in Borneo the annual litter fall weighed only just over six tons, whereas from similar situations in the Amazon basin and Africa it averaged over twelve tons. However, Borneo has many more lizard species in the forest litter than does Amazonia. This discrepancy is explained by the success of the frog *Eleuthrodactylus,* which is abundant in the forests of tropical America and which has eliminated its tadpole stage so that it can develop without access to ponds or streams. The advantage of not being tied to water has enabled these frogs to compete successfully with terrestrial lizards and even displace many of them. The absence of *Eleuthrodactylus* or other well-adapted terrestrial frogs from Borneo has enabled the local lizards to maintain their supremacy.

While the frogs, lizards, and small insectivorous

mammals feed on the soil fauna, they themselves support the populations of snakes, which are the principal medium-size tropical predators. Snake density is a good index of the overall productivity of a region because snakes feed fairly high up the food chain. A much-discussed paradox is that snake densities increase with altitude and peak at about 5,000 feet (1,500 m).

Daniel Janzen and other workers have made studies of the abundance of insects and other animals at different altitudes. The results are consistent. The upper montane forest at about 5,250 feet (1,600 m), provided that it is not cloud forest, is the most diverse and productive forest in the tropics. The reasons are hardly proven, but the suggested explanation is that although the plants of both the lower montane and lowland rain forests are exposed to sufficient light, water, and warmth for rapid production of sugars the high nighttime temperature demands that cellular respiration also continues unabated. At the higher levels the daytime productivities are as high as at lower altitudes, but the significantly cooler nights retard the respiratory rate so that the overall gain by the plant is greater.

Thus, at higher altitudes more energy can be invested in leaf, flower, fruit, and root production. Stated more formally, although gross productivity is high at all sites, net productivity (gross productivity minus losses due to cellular respiration) is higher at the increased altitudes. Higher net productivity means greater litter fall, which not only supports a richer litter fauna by supplying more food but provides more opportunity for concealment and diversification of the fauna. The specialized conditions of the cloud forest are less productive than other forests at similar altitudes because the interruption of the light by the clouds and the reduced temperatures due to the excessive evaporation reduce the rate of photosynthesis. Lower root temperatures may also impede the uptake of soil nutrients.

In regions of high productivity, there is not only a larger mass of herbivores, but of carnivores too, even top carnivores such as cats and birds of prey. There are no large cats prowling the lowland rain forests of the Amazon, but at higher levels in Venezuela, Colombia, Ecuador, Peru, and Bolivia there are pumas, ocelots, and numerous other small carnivores, all supported, ultimately, by the forest trees.

By human standards, all the animals considered so far are small, but they make up for deficiency in size by their numerical abundance. Large animals are never common on the rain-forest floor; there are no grazing animals, such as horses, because of the paucity of herbs and ground cover. Only animals that are able to browse, such as the antelope, can find food supplies, and even resources for these are restricted.

In Africa, the ancestral antelopes were plains grazers but the expansion of rain forests in recent times attracted a number of antelope species. Their forest descendants now include duikers (*Cephalophus*) and chevrotains (*Tragulus*). Small size seems to be an advantage, for rain-forest antelopes are all dwarf by comparison with their

Left. *This* Phenacosaurus *from Colombia has been caught in the act of eating an insect. Arboreal lizards are important insect predators in the rain forest and eat a wide spectrum of prey. However, they cannot be labeled as "good" or "bad" as far as human economics are concerned, for these opportunistic predators are as likely to eat a pollinator as a herbivore. The use of insectivorous animals as agents of biological control of agricultural pests must be based on a sound knowledge of the biology of the predator and the pest. Many errors have been made in the introduction of potentially beneficial predators whose biology was inadequately known.*

Above. *The pangolins have both terrestrial and arboreal representatives in Southeast Asia and Africa. They are the ecological equivalent of the New World anteaters and when disturbed they roll up into a ball, protected externally by their reptilelike scales.*

plains-dwelling counterparts. The royal antelope of West Africa (*Neotragus pygmaeus*) is the smallest antelope known, being little heavier than a rabbit, and the forest antelopes of the Cameroons (*Hylarnus batesi*) and the Semliki forest in western Uganda (*H. harrisoni*) are only a little larger. The forest hippopotamus (*Choeropsis liberiensis*) is also a pygmy, as are the native humans of the Congo. Presumably, small size facilitates movement through the forest, cuts down on food requirements, and offsets the disadvantage of being unable to forage very high. Food materials are either close to the ground or at a great distance from it.

The alternative to small size seems to be the other extreme, for the elephant (*Loxodonta africana*) is a frequent visitor to the rain forest from habitats outside. The tracks made by the elephants are used as a guide by other animals and usually lead to favorite forest sites, known as "elephant tangles" because of the rich secondary growth that follows the disturbance of the habitat by the elephants.

Apart from the duikers, chevrotains, and elephants, the only other large inhabitants of the African rain-forest floor are the rarely seen bongo (*Boocercus eurycerus*), dwarf bushcow (*Syncerus caffer*), bushpigs (*Hylochoerus*), riverhogs (*Potamochoerus*), and okapi (*Okapia johnstoni*). Swamp habitats support the marshbuck (*Limnotragus spekei*), bushbuck (*Tragelaphus scriptus*), and the pygmy hippopotamus (*Choeropsis liberiensis*). The water courses may be inhabited by hippopotamuses (*Hippopotamus amphibius*), manatees (*Trichechus*), and crocodiles (*Crocodylus*), but these animals are more common in rivers that pass through open forests. Rhinoceroses are grazing animals that are typical of the savannas, not the rain forests of Africa. The only large cat likely to be found is the leopard, and then only as an immigrant from the drier forests.

Forest animals are even less abundant in Southeast Asia than in Africa. Species of *Tragulus* are near relatives of the chevrotains of Africa and are presumably parallel descendants since the separation of the two forest systems some fifteen million years ago. Similarly, the Indian elephant (*Elephas maximus*) is closely related to its counterpart in Africa. The rhinoceroses from Southeast Asia have differentiated into three recognizable types, two of which would be in the rain forest if they could be found. All are endangered and are hunted principally for the totally unwarranted superstition that powdered rhino horn is a powerful aphrodisiac. The Sumatran rhinoceros (*Didermocerus sumatrensis*) is native to Borneo (Sabah), Sumatra, Burma, and Malaya, and the Java rhino (*Rhinoceros soudaicus*) is restricted to the northwestern tip of Java.

An anomaly in the close affinity of Southeast Asian and African fauna is the occurrence of the tapir (*Tapiris indicus*), which is the ecological equivalent of the African okapi in Thailand and Sumatra. The only other living tapirs are in Central and South America, although their fossil record in many parts of North America and Eurasia goes back more than twenty-five million years. The tapirs of tropical America and Southeast Asia are the last survivors of a long and successful line. The North American tapir became extinct, along with many other large mammals, about twelve thousand years ago. We are now seeing them in the twilight of their existence, for they are being hunted ruthlessly wherever they occur.

In a comparison of rain-forest mammals on Barro Colorado Island and other localities in South America, John Eisenberg and Richard Thorington of the Smithsonian Institution in Washington list few ground dwellers, and with the exception of the tapir and some deer, they are all small. Their list includes the following vegetarians with their "guestimate" of the average number of animals per acre given in parentheses: collared peccary, *Tayassu tajacu* (0.05); agouti, *Dasyprocta punctata* (0.05); spiny rat, *Proechimys semispinosus* (1.0); paca, *Agouti paca* (?); brocket deer, *Mazama* species (?); white-tailed deer, *Odocoileus* species (?); tapir, *Tapirus bairdii* (0.02); and the insectivorous armadillo, *Dasypus novencincta* (2.0). Notice the overall poverty of the ground fauna and the almost complete absence of terrestrial carnivores. The only carnivore that is sufficiently abundant to be listed is the armadillo, which feeds on insects. However, although only about 30 percent of the total mammal fauna lives on the forest floor, the agouti and spiny rat are important in the recycling of forest litter.

The feeding habits of rain-forest herbivores are probably exemplified by the findings of Valerie Terwilliger, who studied Baird's tapir on Barro Colorado Island in Panama. The present range of American tapirs is the rain forests of Central and South America from Guatemala to western Ecuador, Brazil, and along the Andes of Colombia, Ecuador, and Peru. Terwilliger found that Baird's tapir feeds on ninety-five species of plant and includes fruits, twigs, flowers, and leaves in its diet. Foliage is reached by standing on its hind legs, goat style, but each leaf is bitten once only. The tapir's maxim seems to be "little and often," a feeding technique that would avoid taking in toxic levels of any single plant poison.

A comparison of the terrestrial mammals of Africa and South America shows remarkable similarities in ecological role, even though the animals themselves are quite different. The following pairs of animals fill similar ecological niches, the African animal being listed first: okapi and tapir, pygmy hippo and capybara, chevrotain and paca, royal antelope and agouti, yellow-backed duiker and brocket deer, terrestrial pangolin and giant armadillo. Each of these pairs of animals, although similar in habits, represents two separate families, reminding us that although the two continents have had different histories, the ecological opportunities within the rain forests are basically similar everywhere.

The visits into the edges of the forest by the inhabitants of the savannas and other neighboring habitats causes a crowding effect at the forest margin, for few forest animals venture out beyond the forest limits. This crowding at the forest margins in one of the principal reasons why the tropical rain-forest fauna has been consistently

Following pages. (top left) Corallus caninus, the emerald tree boa from Amazonas, is one of the most beautiful boids. Reaching about five feet long (1.5 m), these snakes are quick to bite and although there is no venom they can inflict multiple lacerations with their hundred or so sharp teeth.

(top right) The sun-flecked forest floor is a mosaic of color in which it is easy for an animal to conceal itself. This viper is alert and ready to strike. Animals that seem gaudy and conspicuous in the hand or in the laboratory may blend into invisibility on the forest floor. Vipers, such as this one in Sri Lanka, usually feed on small mammals.

(bottom) The fer-de-lance (Bothrops atrox) may reach over nine feet long (2.8 m) and must be ranked very dangerous. Usually found near water, they are not commonly found in trees. Notice the pit between the eye and the nostril, an identifying feature of pit vipers (Crotalinae) which is a heat receptor that detects the warmth given out by mammalian prey at night. The organ has an effective range of about three feet.

(right) The várzea of the Amazon basin is annually flooded but during the relatively dry season is a network of small streams. The water is crystal clear, for the currents are slow and there is little silt. It is in these regions that one would find anacondas, the giant water boas, although it is doubtful that there are many reaching the record length of 38 feet (11.6 m).

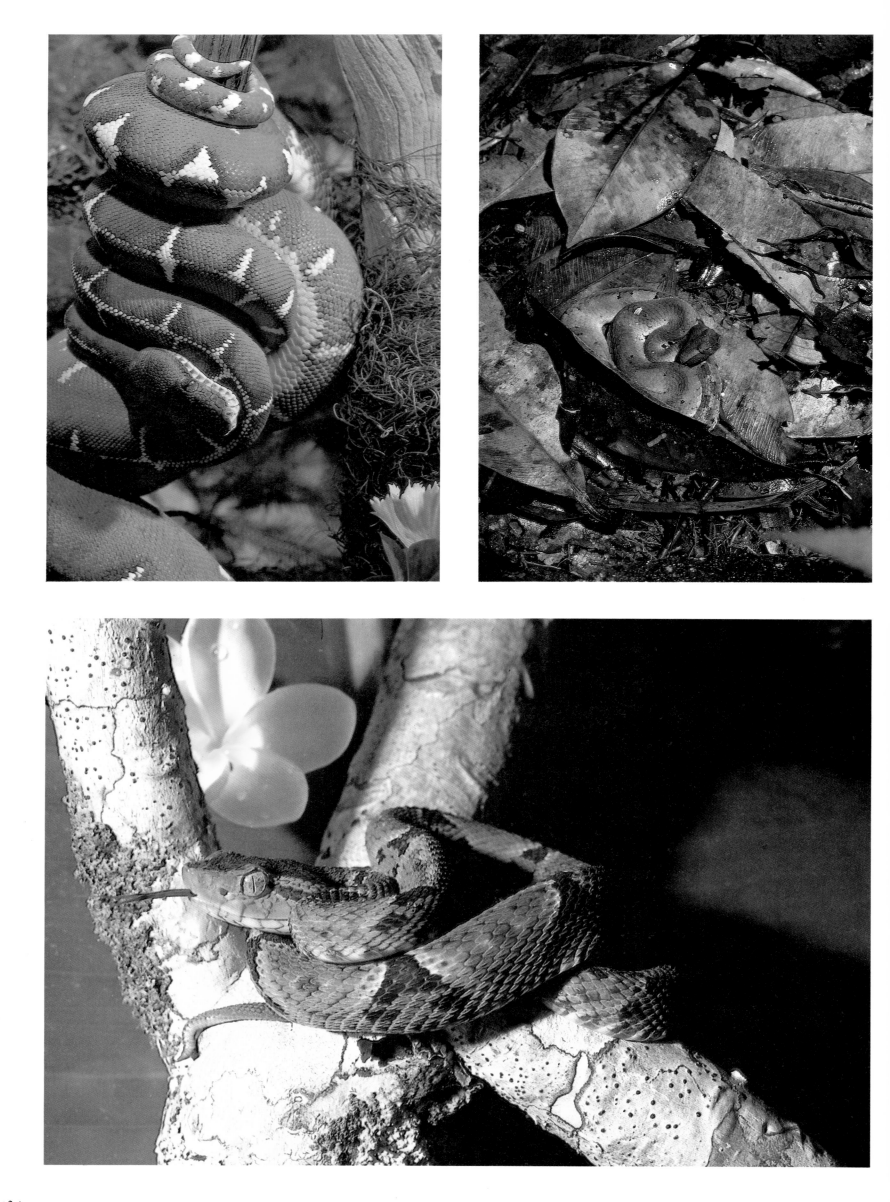

Right. (top) *The Mexican red brocket deer is one of ten species of* Mazama *that inhabit the tropical forests of Central and South America. These tiny, delicate animals are the American equivalent of the African forest duiker. Usually solitary or paired, they emerge from under fallen logs and subterranean retreats only in the evening and early morning. The most conspicuous feature of these secretive animals is the white alarm flag that is exposed when their tails are upturned.*

(top center) Calotes calotes *(Agamidae) is an arboreal lizard of the rain forests of Sri Lanka that feeds on insects and may reach a length of nearly 18 inches (5 cm). The common name "bloodsucker" is derived from the color change undergone by males in ritualistic combat, which begins with the antagonists doing "push-ups." Next, extending their throat fans and turning sideways, they expose the full extent of their body to their opponent. They display closer and closer toward each other until one male concedes the competition and retires a light shade of gray. The front end of the victor turns a deep orange-red and, following the infliction of a bite, forms the foundation of the myth that these lizards are suckers of blood.*

(bottom center) *The boa constrictor* (Boa constrictor) *of Central and South America is the most popular pet among snake fanciers. Inhabiting varied habitats in the wild, from semi-desert to rain forest, these snakes are very tractable in captivity. Specimens up to 9 feet long (2.7 m) can be handled safely without assistance, but beyond that length the constricting coils of the body and tail can become unmanageable. Even experienced snake handlers have been strangled by their pets. The longest recorded specimen was over 18.5 feet long (5.6 m), and one captive snake lived for 23 years.*

(bottom) *The African twig or vine snake* (Thelothornis kirtlandii) *is an innocuous-looking, slender snake, which is known to have caused the death of at least one human. These snakes live in trees and sway the head and neck as if blown by the wind. The black-tipped orange-red tongue is thrust out to lure frogs, lizards, and birds, which identify it as an insect. The horizontal pupils extend so far around the front of the snout that the snake can focus both eyes simultaneously on the prey and strike with unerring accuracy.*

overestimated by travelers and explorers.

The sharpest boundary between the forest and the other ecosystems is at the water's edge. The white water rivers and streams that course through the rain forests are rich with aquatic life. The rivers of Southeast Asia have given us gourami and Siamese fighting fish while the tropical American waterways have yielded mollies, guppies, tetras, swordtails, and many of the other piscatorial delights which are the fish-fancier's stock-in-trade. The cerebral ecstasy of physiologists who marvel at fishes' use of electric fields for the nocturnal detection of near neighbors is matched only by the satisfaction of pronouncing such names as *Gymnorhamphichthys* correctly!

Whenever I think of tropical fish I become affected by just a twinge of guilt. In Trinidad, a colleague and I used to help raise money for the local school at their annual fête. As children approached our aquarium booth we would invite them to buy and net a swordtail for ten cents. If they were not satisfied with the fish they caught they were encouraged to replace it and catch another for an additional five cents. The tank contained eye-catching bright red males and drab-colored females, recently taken from a nearby stream. Of course, the kiddies always caught a male, which was then transferred into a water-filled transparent plastic bag for the journey home. The shock of being netted almost always caused the fish to lose their color, so within minutes the child would return to trade the fish in for another more brilliant specimen. Each fish realized about twenty cents in initial purchase price plus levies for exchange! Every time I hear a remark abut the kind of person who would steal a child's Saturday pocket money, my stomach gives me a memory-tweaking cramp.

Our knowledge of tropical fish and other aquatic organisms is rudimentary. The rivers of South America have the richest fauna of any aquatic system in the world, yet the biology of very few species is known. Even waters that seem relatively unproductive in terms of algae and other aquatic plants can support substantial fish populations by the fruit fall from riverain trees. We are barely at the edge of our understanding of the relationship between the organisms of the waterways and the animals and plants of the forest floor.

Following pages. *There is no doubt that the schools of voracious charcin fish in the rivers of South America are to be feared, but the meat-eating skills of the piranha are exaggerated. These fish are unusual in that they have teeth that are specialized for different purposes, whereas it is usual for fish teeth to be uniform in shape and no more than graduated in size.*

Above. *The duikers of tropical African rain forests are small secretive creatures, as exemplified by* Cephalophus zebra, *the zebra duiker or stripe-backed duiker of West Africa. Duikers usually are found alone or in pairs, and are nocturnal and shy. Duiker, translated from Afrikaans, means "diving buck," after the way in which they dive into the thickest vegetation when disturbed.*

Opposite. (top) *No apology is needed for the captivity of this Sumatran rhinoceros (*Didermocerus sumatrensis), *for in its native haunts of Thailand, Borneo, Sumatra, and the Malay Peninsula it is near extinction. It is one of the few rain-forest rhinoceroses and is the smallest, with a height at the shoulder which rarely exceeds 4½ feet(1.5 m). The horns of rhinoceroses, which are made of compacted hair, have gained the reputation of being powerful aphrodisiacs when taken orally as a finely ground powder. This quite unwarranted claim has accelerated the demise of these fabulous animals.*

Right. *Once worldwide in distribution, lemurs are now confined to the island of Madagascar, while the lorises, their near relatives, are found only in Southeast Asia. Lemurs are presently severely threatened by habitat destruction and by hunting for food and sale. The ringtailed lemur (*Lemur catta) *here is popular with zoos and as pets, for it is readily tamed and will feed on a variety of fruit. Even though this example was photographed in a Madagascan rain forest, these lemurs are more characteristic of the open arid regions.*

Left. *The clouded leopard* (Neofelis nebulosa) *is one of the few large cats that inhabits the rain forest of Southeast Asia and Indonesia, and is almost exclusively arboreal and nocturnal. Little is known of its biology in the wild and only a few specimens have reached Western zoos. The upper canine teeth are proportionally the longest of all modern cats and approach the length of those of the extinct sabre-toothed tigers.*

Above. *Jaguars* (Panthera onca) *are the heaviest cats in the Americas and are the ecological equivalent of the Old World leopards. Jaguars are still fairly common in riverain rain forests at moderate elevations, although they are continuously hunted for their hides and because of their attacks on domesticated animals. Their diet is varied and even includes alligators and fish. In more open and drier country, the jaguar is replaced by the puma, which is known as the cougar in North America.*

The Ubiquitous Ants

Ants are, perhaps, the most unavoidable insects of the tropical forest. Everywhere you look there are ants busying themselves—scouting, lumbering, sewing, milking, fighting, foraging, or laying trails. Among the most remarkable terrestrial ants are the parasol and army ants of South and Central America, the driver ants of Africa and Asia, and the various ants that have gone into partnership with plants. These insects have rich, fascinating lives and are worth considering in detail.

When Henry W. Bates first saw the parasol ants of the genus *Atta* and *Acromyrex* (also known as leaf-cutter and fungus-garden ants) about 1850 in Amazonia, he thought they gathered pieces of leaf "to thatch the domes which cover the entrance to the subterranean dwellings thereby protecting from the deluging rains the young brood in the nests beneath." About 1870, another naturalist, Thomas Belt, working in Nicaragua, discovered the truth. The leaves and petals cropped by the ants are used only as a medium upon which to cultivate the fungus *Rozites gonglyophora,* which forms the staple of their diet.

The fungus culture originates with the queen ant that founds the colony. Once mated, she bites off her wings, excavates a suitable site, and deposits a mass of fungus-infected culture medium which she gathered from the parent colony before taking off on her nuptial flight. Armed with the key to her colony's survival, she begins to lay eggs, eating some of them herself and feeding others to her first-hatched nymphs. The first few broods to become mature are sexless, wingless workers that now busy themselves cleaning, excavating, foraging, and tending to the needs of the queen. As the number of workers increases, the queen becomes totally confined to the royal chamber, where she becomes an egg-laying machine for up to twenty years. The sperm, stored within her body after the honeymoon flight, will be released gradually over the next few years so that without further need for a mate she will lay many millions of fertilized eggs.

During the early stages of the development of the colony, but after substantial numbers of workers have been produced, some of the developing nymphs acquire enormous heads and formidable mandibles. This sexless, wingless caste has the function of defending the nest against invaders such as other ants, anteaters, and entomologists. These soldiers stand guard at the entrance and attack any intruder, no matter what its size. Investigators excavating their nests rarely escape without being severely bitten. The mandibles of the soldiers can penetrate all but the hardest and thickest human skin. The naturalist William Beebe used to protect himself by wearing tall boots covered with grease, but that was rarely adequate, for it was not long before the later arrivals could climb over the bodies of their comrades and attack living skin.

The soldiers are so tenacious that once firmly embedded in the skin, the rest of the insect can be cut away from the head without the grip being released. Stories, which are probably true, are told about soldier ants that have been used to clamp gaping human wounds and with the bodies removed the heads have held the skin together while it healed! Even if true, these instances would not be the only occasions in which insects have been used directly in the course of medicine, for during the building of the Panama Canal it is said that the light from luminous beetles (*Pyrophorus,* Elateridae) was used to illuminate a successful surgical operation.

The colonies of *Atta,* which may contain up to one million individuals, are almost totally underground, but the excavated soil is piled up on top so that there is usually a mound of bare earth up to twenty or thirty feet across (6–9 m). No seeds are allowed to germinate on top of the mound. From holes at the base of the mound, broad, smooth paths up to eight inches wide radiate out into the forest for distances of up to half a mile. Usually, ants can be seen energetically trotting along the paths, unencumbered on the way out but returning laden with a piece of leaf or petal, which is grasped in the mandibles and held over the back in the manner of a parasol.

The workers know their tasks well. Many times every day, each worker will forage for plant tissue with which to prepare the fungus gardens. In the dry season of the deciduous forest, when the overhead foliage is more scanty and flecks of direct sunlight form a broad mosaic on the forest floor, the ants forage only at night, for to be caught exposed in even a sun fleck can lead to overheating, immobility, and death. Only during the rainy season, when the overhead canopy is dense, is foraging carried out by both day and night.

One would think that the ants would defoliate all the trees in the near neighborhood of their nest, but they are superb conservationists. Larry Rockwood, of George Mason University in Virginia, has shown that the ants take only a small proportion of the foliage of any one tree, so they do not destroy the sources of their own nourishment. They go hundreds of meters to productive sites far away from the nest.

As the older leaves often have higher levels of protective poisons, it is the younger leaves, which have not had sufficient time to produce adequate levels, that are favored by the leaf cutters. The choice of leaves is important to the ants and often demands that foraging cover a very large area. Petals are harvested during dry seasons when young leaves are in short supply. The harvested vegetation is chewed with saliva and mixed with an anal secretion before being added to the fungus garden. There is difference of opinion about the nature of the origin of the material on which the ants actually feed. Some observers believed that the ants fed only on fruiting bodies, which they alleged were unobtainable in the laboratory cultures. Neal Weber, at Swarthmore College in Pennsylvania, made a lifelong study of these fungus gardeners and maintains that the knobby structures of the fungi, upon which all observers agree that the ants feed, appear in laboratory cultures in the absence of the ants. Others believe that the knobs only

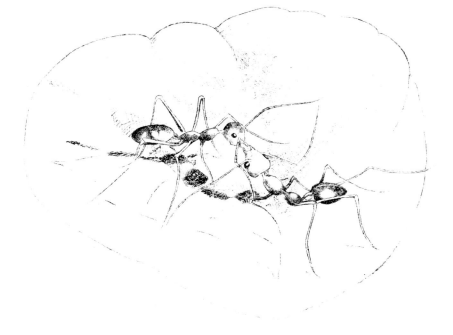

appear in response to mutilation of the fungal threads by the ants. Perhaps the final resolution will be that there is genuinely great variation in the behavior of both the ants and the fungi from species to species, or even from colony to colony. It does seem universally true that the ants prevent the growth of other, inedible fungi, for whenever a nest is abandoned by the ants the fungus gardens are rapidly overtaken by foreign fungi. For a long time it was thought that the ants produced a specific fungicide that cleansed the gardens of invaders, but no such substance has been isolated in spite of vigorous searching.

In time of food shortage the queen's eggs are eaten, an adaptation that serves the double purpose of providing nourishment for the existing brood and preventing any further buildup of the population. These cannibalistic habits are exceptional, for normally the ants are not aggressive toward members of their own species.

When the workers of one colony meet those of another, there is rarely conflict, just the demarcation of an imaginary line that forms the boundaries of each colony's foraging territories. Both colonies keep to their side of the boundary; however, if one colony is particularly successful, its superior growth will demand the gradual expansion of its territory and corresponding loss by its neighbors. These territorial gains are usually accomplished by superior numbers of workers at the boundary, the larger numbers meeting little resistance as they push their neighbors back.

Stories are told of ants carrying their injured colleagues back to the nest, but these are rarely documented. However, Hubert Markl, now at Konstanz University in West Germany, has shown that if there is a collapse of soil inside the nest, the buried workers tap with their abdomens so their fellows will know where they are and will be able to dig them out. Markl demonstrated the method of communication by having each leg of the ants stand on a loudspeaker cone that emitted a recording of the abdominal taps. Only the front leg below the subgenual organ was capable of initiating nervous impulses to the brain in response to the taps.

Dead ants, remains of intruders, and refuse from the fungus gardens are all carried out of the nest and dumped either at special places used only for that purpose or in a nearby stream. Ants have been seen climbing an overhanging tree limb and dropping their waste into the running water of a forest stream from above. The removal of waste and the burying of vast quantities of vegetation in the underground nests have a substantial influence on the distribution of nutrients on the forest floor. The fungus gardeners are, perhaps, the only animals that draw plant material down to a substantial depth below the litter layer. They are the tropical ecological equivalent of earthworms.

The parasol ants, in common with most ant species, have a permanent nesting site which may remain active for many years. At least one knows where to find the ants, so long-term studies can be planned with confidence. No such convenience awaits the student of army or driver ants. In

Opposite. These ants are probably on their way to "milk" their domesticated aphids. The ants protect the aphids in exchange for a sugary secretion known as honeydew. They are climbing on the roots of the familiar houseplant Philodendron *that are clamped tightly to the bark of their support.*

Above. *These ants on a jackfruit are attending their domesticated treehopper nymphs (Membracidae), which secrete sugary honeydew much apprecated by ants. In exchange, the ants protect them from predators and parasites.*

Right. *Honeydew-seeking ants are attending treehopper nymphs. One nymph and an adult have a parasitic red mite attached to them.*

Central and South America, *Eciton* and *Neivamyrmex* live in colonies of several hundred thousand to more than a million individuals without a permanent nest. Their temporary dwellings are made of thousands of worker ants each holding onto the legs of their neighbors by their mandibles and claws. Gigantic bivouacs, up to a cubic meter in size, are made entirely of interlocking ants. Within this protective structure resides the queen and the colony's developing brood. In most species the assembly of the bivouac is a daily event, each nighttime being spent in forced march in search of new food supplies. However, periodically the daily marching is discontinued and a semipermanent bivouac is established. From this central location daily raiding parties sally forth and return with their booty. Then the stationary phase of their life is over and the daily marching begins again.

The duration of the long-term rhythms of the colony depends on the time taken for the development of the larvae, for while there are larvae in the colony, their secretions, which are exchanged for food, stimulate the colony to march, at night only, for about two and a half to three weeks. While on the march, a colony of eighty thousand adults and thirty thousand larvae need about a half-gallon of "meat" a day. Their food supplies are acquired by having scouts lead the way and signal with an odor when large caches of prey have been found. Small animals are killed and brought back to the central marching column entire or dismembered, according to size. Immobilized large animals, even up to the size of a tethered donkey, have been killed and dismembered by thousands of ants recruited by the scouts' signals. There are many undocumented stories of humans being killed by army ants, but except for babies or the infirm, most humans are sufficiently mobile to escape, for the speed of the advancing ants is little faster than a few meters per hour. However, the ability to bite and sting simultaneously makes them formidable adversaries.

When the larvae are fully developed, they prepare to pupate and cease their secretion of stimulant, and the bivouac becomes semipermanent. For a period of three weeks the colony rests, waiting for the pupae to mature and emerge as new adults. However, at a carefully timed point during the resting period the queen lays about twenty-five to thirty thousand eggs over a two-day period. Just after the pupae have emerged, the eggs hatch and the young larvae begin secreting "marching substance"—the colony is on the move once more. While bivouacked, the food needs of the colony are somewhat modest, for the brood is in the nonfeeding egg or pupal stages. It is while on the march and while feeding their larvae that food requirements become so high. The larvae are carried in the jaws of workers during the marches and are found toward the middle of the column. Some species, such as the so-called legionary ant (*E. rapax*), march in single file while other species (*E. burchelli*) may have a front up to sixty-six feet (20 m) wide. No food is ignored. While standing still in the forest, the noise of the advancing column can be heard distinctly as the ants rustle and rattle the leaves. The "plopping and plinking" of jumping insects is masked by the noise of birds picking off the escapees in the air. Some observers claim to be able to hear the buzzing of parasitic flies, which attack the ants and lay eggs in their bodies.

The armies are unstoppable. On reaching a stream, the first arrivers interlock their claws and float out on the water. Soon, there is a ropelike raft of living ants drifting downstream. Ultimately the lead ant touches the other side, whereupon it takes hold and anchors itself securely. The ant rope is wound in until it forms an almost direct connection across the width of the stream. Other ants reinforce the sides of the pontoon until it is wide enough to accommodate the marching column, which then proceeds to tramp over the floating or partially submerged bodies of the living bridge. It is inevitable that many ants are drowned or flushed downstream, but their numbers are soon restored with new broods.

In contrast to these highly visible army ants, the blind driver ants *Dorylus, Aenictus,* and *Anomma* of Africa and Southeast Asia are normally hidden under the forest litter and exposed only when crossing a road or bare patch of earth. Columns have been estimated to contain twenty-two million individuals. During certain times of the year, the flying reproductive stages are attracted to lights and are known as "sausage flies" because of their large, robust abdomens. They are considered a gourmet delicacy by many native tribes and are eaten lightly toasted over a fire. In Nigeria I was told that they, along with beetle grubs and grasshoppers, were almost tasteless but left a lingering fatty residue in the mouth.

Investigations by Edward Wilson, Bert Hölldobler, and William Gotwald have been responsible for much of our knowledge of army and driver ants. Similarly, the story of the acacia and cecropia ants that follows has been exposed by the seasonal studies of Daniel Janzen and Jerry Downhower. The acacia and cecropia ant relationships are so extraordinary that they are now discussed in almost every introductory biology textbook.

The bullhorn acacia tree (*Acacia cornigera:* Leguminosae) of Central and South America is equipped with huge hornlike thorns which arise in opposing pairs along the stem. When the thorns are mature they are soft-centered and are soon perforated and hollowed out by a *Pseudomyrmex* queen ant. In the confines of her thorn the queen raises her brood, but to accommodate her enlarging family, her workers excavate other thorns until each one on the tree is utilized. The *Acacia* provides not only housing, but nourishment, too, for arising from the stem at the base of each leaf are globular structures containing high concentrations of protein and fat, which are harvested by the ants and used to feed both the adults and their larvae. In recognition of their discoverer, Thomas Belt, they are known as Beltian bodies.

In exchange for the services provided by the plant, the

Following pages. *Weaver ants are most common in Southeast Asia, the Indonesian islands, and here in northern Australia. The larvae of these ants produce silk for nest building. The adults hold adjacent leaves together with their feet while other adults hold larvae in their jaws and, squeezing gently, stimulate silk production from the larvae mouths. Touching the edges of the leaves with a zig-zag motion of the tacky silk, the adults sew the leaves together into a tightly bound weatherproof nest.*

Opposite. (top) *Leaf-cutting ants, a common sight in tropical American rain forests, scurry along with their burden of a piece of leaf or petal held over their backs, parasol-style. They do not eat the material they gather, but use it to prepare a compost bed on which they cultivate a fungus which forms their principal food. These* Atta *workers are harvesting leaves in Belém, Brazil.*

(center left) *The leaves in the nests of the West African weaver ant,* Oecophylla longinoda, *are more frequently rolled than those of other species. In the rolling of the leaves, the workers form chains by gripping their neighbors' feet in their mandibles and forming a living winch which can pull distant leaves together to be glued with larval silk.*

(center right) *It is very difficult to avoid anthropomorphism when considering the ways of the ant. The colonies of the Ghanaian weaver ant illustrated have castes whose duties range from defense by the soldiers and egg production by the queen, to foraging, child-care, nest construction, and garbage collection by the workers. However, in contra-distinction to human societies, the ants' activities are all instinctive. They have such little control over their behavioral programs that they are truly robots.*

(bottom) *Once the weaver ants' abode has been completed, the nest may be colonized by a moth, whose caterpillars spin a waterproof lining over the inside. That these caterpillars are tolerated by the ants is only surprising when one learns of the high price that the caterpillars exact for their constructional skill — they feed on the developing ant larvae! These* Oecophylla smaragdina *workers are from Magnetic Island, off the coast of Queensland, Australia.*

ants constantly patrol the leaves and keep the foliage completely clean of caterpillars and other small herbivores. Even browsing goats are deterred by the aggressive stings of the ants. Furthermore, the ants nip off the growing points of any climbing vines which come within reach but which have not yet gained a tendrilhold.

The mutualistic relationship is finely balanced. In return for the investment in the thorns and nutrients, the plant is allowed to grow unencumbered by vines and parasitic herbivores. The plant may also have to make a smaller investment in protective chemicals, for it has been shown experimentally that the mature leaves are palatable to some caterpillars. The thorns of the *Acacia* are sometimes occupied by *Pseudomyrmex nigripilosa,* an ant which does not patrol the foliage and which gives the plant no protection in exchange for the services provided. This parasitic ant is evicted by the beneficial *Pseudomyrmex* whenever it is encountered!

In the lowland forests of the Cameroons in Africa, Doyle McKey has recently described a similar relationship between *Leonardoxa africana* (Caesalpiniaceae) and a species of an *Acromyrmex* ant. However, in this case the mature leaves are chemically well protected and have a long life of about two years, compared with the six months in *Acacia.* Is it coincidence that in this relationship the ants patrol only the young, unprotected leaves? Let us examine another example.

All over tropical America, disturbed forests are colonized by *Cecropia* (Moraceae), a fast-growing tree that is favored by high light intensities. The species studied most thoroughly is *Cecropia peltata,* which occurs in both Central and South American forests and some West Indian islands below about 8,200 feet (2,500 m).

Cecropia has hollow stems that are penetrated at a circular area of weakness just above each leaf origin by *Azteca* ants. The ants use the stems as nesting sites for raising their brood and as protective "barns," where their honeydew-producing bugs can feed without interruption or danger. As in *Acacia,* the plant reinforces the benefits of occupancy by providing nourishment at special structures, termed trichilia. It has been estimated that each trichilium produces between 2,500 and 8,000 nutrient-rich capsules during the 20- to 25-day period that a particular trichilium is operative. The total production of about 90 milligrams of trichilium tissue per day, consisting of about 50 percent energy-rich glycogen, constitutes a significant drain on the plant's resources, for the plant has to build the trichilia, organize the associated biochemistry, and support the ants' guests. The effort must be adequately rewarded or the relationship would not persist. Once again, just as in the case of *Acacia,* the ants keep the foliage clean of insect parasites and will drive away large herbivores with bites from their powerful mandibles. It is interesting to note that on Caribbean islands and at altitudes above about 6,560 feet (2,000 m) where the *Azteca* ants are absent, the *Cecropia* does not produce trichilia.

Opposite. (top) *Honeydew is produced by the sap-suckers for ants as a feeding by-product. In order to extract adequate quantities of protein, sap-suckers have to process inordinately large volumes of carbohydrate-rich fluid. They have put these wastes to good use by bartering them for protection by ants. The ants stimulate the anal flow of the honeydew by caressing their domesticates with their antennae. The captives shown here are scale insects on a* Heliconia *plant in Cibodja, Java.*

(center) *These ants from Ghana are feeding on a caterpillar that they have found and killed. Nearly all ants are at least partially predatory and their vast numbers exercise significant control over the populations of insects in the vicinity of their nests.*

Left. *"Ant's eggs," such as those used as fish food, are really the ants' pupae (a resting stage between larva and adult). Whenever the colony is disturbed, assigned nurse workers scurry away, carrying the "eggs" to safety in their jaws. These ants were photographed in Ghana.*

Above. *With mandibles open to almost 180 degrees, the worker ants of* Odontomachus hastatus *are known to grasp a twig or stone and tighten their grip until the mandibles suddenly slip off, whereupon the ant may be projected several centimeters into the air. The function of this strange practice is obscure.*

Regrettably, most of our modern understanding of tropical ants, and indeed tropical biology generally, has been obtained by temperate-based biologists. It is sad that a larger contribution has not been made by biologists who live in the countries inhabited by the organisms. The reason for this inequality is not the indolence of the tropical scientists but the extreme need for applied research in the developing world. Tropical science is directed almost exclusively at solving practical problems in agriculture and medicine. It is the rarely acknowledged privilege of academic freedom that allows the faculty of North American and European universities to study esoteric aspects of basic research. It is understandable that tropical-based biologists are somewhat envious of "northerners" who can fly into a tropical country, pick off the most exciting topics, and return to their homelands to publish the results, while they themselves are immersed in more immediate duties, such as insecticidal programs and the prevention of disease.

Right. *You do not have to live in the tropics to find exciting insect relationships. These captive aphids from Washington, D.C., are being stroked by their carpenter ant masters* (Camponotus pennsylvanicus) *in order to stimulate the production of honeydew. Because of these close domestic relationships, aphids are sometimes referred to as "ant cows."*

Above. *The strong jaws of this* Dinoponera *soldier from Belém, Brazil, can puncture the skin of a person's finger while the other end is inflicting an agonizingly painful sting. These soldiers are the largest ants and may be substantially longer than an inch and a quarter.*

Flowering Strategies

Together, insects, birds, bats, and flowering plants have adapted to meet each other's needs. The plants offer nectar or some other reward for visitation, while the animals unknowingly transfer pollen from flower to flower as they collect their bribes. This interaction is pollination, and plants have developed a wide spectrum of techniques in order to ensure that their flowers are pollinated. The various devices involve timing and position of flower opening, flower shape, and color. These features are collectively known as flowering strategies.

The earliest-known flowering plants date from about 130 million years ago in the Cretaceous period. Animals involved in pollination at that time most likely were beetles and primitive mammals. There is no evidence that bees, wasps, flies, butterflies, or bats existed, and the birds were probably not as strong fliers as they are today.

Each rain-forest plant species has specialized in one of four basic flowering strategies, known to phenologists (students of flowering patterns) as steady state, cornucopia, multiple bang, and big bang. The first strategy, that of steady-state flowering, consists of opening just a few flowers every day throughout the year. This approach to pollination is risky, for the plant may offer insufficient flowers to feed a viable population of pollinators. However, offsetting the risk of not being pollinated at all is the virtual certainty that if any visiting insect is carrying pollen of the same species of plant it will be from a different individual and therefore increase genetic variability in the resultant seeds.

Plants that use the steady-state technique are most commonly specialized for pollination by particular kinds of animals which indulge in daily trapline foraging expeditions. Traplining is a technique used by many tropical bees, hummingbirds, bats, and some butterflies and hawkmoths in which they fly along regular pathways each day, visiting the same tree or bush about the same time. Insects can be caught, marked with an identifiable dab of paint, and released, only to be recaptured at the same site the following day and for many days thereafter. The daily reward for each visit provides habitual reinforcement and therefore makes the flight worthwhile. If the flowering were sporadic, some flights would go unrewarded and that individual plant would be eliminated from the animal's flyway.

Steady-state flowering is most commonly displayed by plants with limited resources, such as C-level trees and lianas. The foliage of these plants is not fully exposed above the canopy, so if their flowers were on the terminal shoots they would not be readily visible to pollinators. These are the plants that usually bear flowers directly on their trunks at the level of the understory. In this position they are clearly visible to potential pollinators.

In contrast to the steady-state strategy in which a few flowers open each day, cornucopia flowering builds up to a peak over a period of several weeks to a month, the tree being without flowers at all for the remainder of the year. This flowering pattern, familiar to most North Americans and Europeans, is characteristic of temperate forests. As success for the plant depends on attracting a wide selection of pollinators, the flowers tend to be relatively unspecialized. The duration of the flowering tends to be longer in those plants which are characteristic of disturbed forests and in the colonizers of light gaps than in the plants of the more mature understory. The reason, presumably, is that this strategy requires a heavy investment of energy to keep the nectar flowing for a long period and only plants exposed to strong light have that level of resource. Furthermore, the flowers must be plainly visible initially, at least, for pollinators are uneducated and have to find the flowers visually.

In the nonseasonal forests the flower production of different cornucopia plant species is usually spread out evenly over the whole year, although there is a question whether any forest is truly nonseasonal. Only the most exceptional forests have insignificant changes in rainfall throughout the year, and peaks of flowering are often associated with changes in rainfall. However, it is vital that the pollinators have a year-round supply of nectar, particularly those pollinators, such as hummingbirds, which are long-lived. If the flowering of the majority of the forest trees were synchronized over a relatively short period of time, then the pollinators would be faced with a feast-or-famine situation. Unlike animal species, which are rarely genetically compatible and hardly ever produce hybrids in the wild, plants that are closely related may hybridize, or outcross, readily. One usually finds that the flowering peaks of closely related species of rain-forest plants occur at different times of the year, so that the chance of hybridization is reduced.

The likelihood of plants being outcrossed is less with the cornucopia strategy because the smaller pollinators can fulfill their nutritional needs from the abundance of flowers on a single plant. However, the larger pollinators are usually strong fliers, so provided the spacing of the individual trees is not too great, the chances of cross-pollination are quite good. The powers of flight of the pollinators will determine just how widely spaced the trees can afford to be. Bat-pollinated canopy trees can be up to a kilometer apart, for such distances are flown regularly by bats, and for large nectar sources one-way flights of about fifteen miles (25 km) are on record. On the other hand, a cacao tree, depending on pollination by the midge *Forcipomyia,* which is only a millimeter long, could become isolated by a distance of a few hundred meters.

Multiple-bang flowering is most often associated with vines and lianas and consists of a small number of explosive bursts of flowering scattered throughout the year. As the duration of the flowering burst may be as short as two days, the chances of outcrossing would be minimal if the flowering of different individuals were not synchronized. In strongly seasonal forests, the flowering trigger is usually the cessation of rain at the onset of the dry season, or the minirains that precede the full power of the rainy season. In some species there is a built-in delay of several weeks or

Left. *This spectacular Brazilian passion flower,* Passiflora coccinea, *has edible fruit but the foliage is protected from many herbivores by highly poisonous cyanide compounds. However, the caterpillars of some butterflies not only eat the leaves but they sequester the poison, which later makes the adult butterflies unpalatable to birds.*

Above. *The clusters of yellow flowers of* Heliconia collinsiana *are rendered conspicuous only because they contrast with the brilliant red bracts.*

months between the activation by the trigger and the floral outburst. In nonseasonal forests, the triggers are often obscure, but rainfall is never absolutely uniform so it is possible that minor variations in precipitation are still the active cues. Changes in daylength must not be overlooked just because the changes are small—a plant in Nigeria has been shown to be sensitive to a daylength change of only fifteen minutes within the whole annual cycle!

Many multiple-bang flowering lianas have their floral displays timed to coincide with the end of the vast output of nearby cornucopia or multiple-bang trees. The immediate advantage is that the liana cashes in on a massive advertising program, for their energy resources are substantially less than that of trees and their display on its own would be rather unimpressive. A nice twist is that in some cases the liana flowers look exactly like tree flowers but contain no nectar! During the flowering of the tree, the pollinators become educated to expect a nectar reward from each visit. With the decline of the tree flowers they enter the liana flowers only to find out that there is consistently no reward, but it is too late—the liana has already been pollinated by their visits. Clearly, such deception can only be successful with precise timing.

The last pattern, known as "big bang," is mass flowering similar to cornucopia in that it takes place only once each year, but which extends for a period of only a few days. These flowers usually depend opportunistically on the presence of pollinators which other plants have sustained during the remainder of the year. Some bees, however, have geared their life cycle to the flowering patterns of big-bang plants and emerge from their underground earthen cells shortly before the big bang. The queen bees mate and prepare their brood cells for the supply of pollen and nectar; then, when the burst of flowering takes place they provision their cells with food supplies, lay their eggs, seal their nests, and die. The brood develops on the food supply and remains in a period of dormancy until triggered to emerge in time for the next bout of feasting. These insect pollinators are active for such a short time and are found in such inaccessible places that we are probably ignorant of the existence of many of them.

The structure, color, and opening time of flowers have to be closely adapted to the needs of the pollinators. Some animals, such as hawkmoths and hummingbirds, hover while feeding and contact the flower only with the tongue and head. The floral structure of flowers visited by these potential pollinators must be appropriate or there will be no pollination. We easily forget that insects can see ultraviolet reflectance as a color, so flowers that to us seem uniform white or red may have a distinctive pattern when perceived by an insect. The flower must also open during the period when pollinators are active, which in some cases may be for periods as short as an hour or even less. Thus, flowering plants have all made unconscious choices whether to be generalized and attract a wide spectrum of pollinators or to be specialized and depend on only a few.

One of the most exhilarating sights in the tropics is the view of the canopy during a burst of dry-season flowering. The paucity of foliage throws open the doors of the finest flower show in the world. The buzzing of the pollinators around the crowns of trees in full bloom can be heard hundreds of yards away.

We normally associate "buzzing" with bees, but before the arrival of the Europeans there were no honeybees *(Apis mellifera)* in the Americas, although there were many native American bees. The earliest date for the introduction of the honeybee seems to be 1532 in Brazil, and by the early 1600s it had been spread to Mexico and other parts of Central America. Experiments have shown that although the honeybee can distinguish the colors blue, yellow, and green, it is blind to red. It is probably not coincidence that the majority of flowers in Africa and the Far East, where honeybees are native, are yellow, blue, and green. The reason that there are more red flowers in the Americas than elsewhere in the tropics is due to the unique presence of hummingbirds, which can see red quite distinctly. The long trumpet-shaped red flowers of the Americas are almost all hummingbird pollinated.

Gary Stiles has studied hummingbird pollination in Costa Rica for many years now and has made the generalization that hermit hummingbirds, which do not defend territories, have long, curved bills and are restricted to the flowers of the understory. Nonhermits, on the other hand, may defend territories and thus range less widely and forage in more varied habitats, including the forest canopy and secondary growth. Hummingbirds are most frequently found in light gaps and at the forest margins, for those are the places where flowers are most abundant. Hummingbirds are long-lived, so hummingbird-pollinated plants have to enable their pollinators to survive all year long, unless the birds are migratory, as is the case with the ruby-throated hummingbird of the eastern United States.

The spectrum of flower pollinators includes hawkmoths, butterflies, bees, wasps, beetles, flies, hummingbirds, and bats. Generally, the largest flowers are pollinated by the largest animals, which are bats, while the smallest flowers are pollinated by the smallest insects. This association is logical, for the largest animals need the largest nectar reward for each visit. The magnitude of the nectar reward has to be a perfect compromise: sufficient to make the visit worthwhile to the pollinator, yet not enough to satisfy the animal's needs too quickly, for the sole objective of offering nectar is to attract a pollinator that has already visited another flower, preferably on a different plant. The ideal nectar supply would just, but only just, make the visit worthwhile.

The energy requirements of hovering animals such as hummingbirds, hawkmoths, and American bats are so great that the nectar has to be copious and rich. The danger is then that other pollinators, whose needs are less, may also visit the flowers and lower the efficiency of the pollination mechanism. Thus, it is to exclude such unwelcome visitors

Opposite. Combretum grandiflorum *is a native of West Africa but has been cultivated for many years. A rambling shrub with whiplike branches, its habit of climbing high into trees and covering them with a sheet of flaming inflorescences has given rise to its common name "burning bush."*

Above. Aeschynanthus *from Kota Kinabalu is similar to the popular houseplant A.* javanicus, *the lipstick plant, so-called because before the red flowers open they lie enclosed within the tubular green or purple calyx and resemble an unextended lipstick.*

Left. Bixa orellana, *the lipstick tree, is one of the most photographed trees of the rain forest, for the intense red of the fruits attracts every traveler with a camera. The tree is native to tropical America and the West Indies but is now widely distributed throughout the tropics.*

Opposite. (top left) The fruits and flowers of palms are rarely spectacular because they lack brilliant colors. For many years botanists considered the palms to be primarily wind pollinated but recent research suggests that small inconspicuous insects play an important role in many palm species. The palm shown here is Caryota mitis *from Indonesia.*

(top right) The large lady palm (Rhapsis excelsa) *from southern China is a miniature fan palm with bamboolike canes and is widely used as a potted ornamental. However, it is doubtful that potted specimens ever produce the rich inflorescence seen here.*

(bottom) The breadfruit, Artocarpus atilis, *is native to Polynesia, where it has been the staple food of the inhabitants since ancient times. Descriptions of the plant were brought back to Europe by Captain Cook and others, so in 1789 Captain William Bligh was sent by King George III to Tahiti to collect the plants and transport them to the West Indies, where they were to be used to feed the slaves. The mutiny on the* Bounty *negated that attempt, but in an expedition three years later the mission was accomplished. The original tree was still growing in the botanical garden in St. Vincent in 1966.*

that plants have developed flowers of specialized shapes and open them only at restricted times when their pollinators are in flight. For example, hummingbird flowers in the Americas are drawn out into elongate tubes of narrow diameter to exclude bees and other large-bodied insects. The flowers are red, a color that is particularly easy for birds to distinguish but difficult for bees, and the flower hangs down at a slight angle to the horizontal so that only hummingbirds, which hover with their heads upraised, can probe the nectaries with their tongues. With these precautions the flower can afford to offer a substantial amount of nectar with a high sugar content, but as an additional insurance the nectar is secreted only at those times during which the hummingbirds are on the wing. Herbert Baker, of the University of California at Berkeley, reported that the nectar of hummingbird-pollinated flowers is usually about 23 percent sugar. If the solution were weaker, he argues, it would not be worth the birds' effort to seek the flowers, hover, and extract it. If the solution were stronger it would be too viscous for the birds to extract. Twenty-three percent is just right.

Opening time is a technique which limits the flower visitors substantially. Hawkmoth-pollinated flowers usually open at dusk to coincide with the flight periods of these insects. Similarly, bat-pollinated flowers open after dark or at dusk and close soon after midnight when the bats return to their roost. In Africa and Southeast Asia the bats do not hover while visiting flowers, as they do in the Americas. So we find that whereas American bat-pollinated flowers are relatively small, bell-shaped, and designed to be visited from below, the Old World bat-pollinated flowers are commonly spherical and are visited by the bat landing on the flower stalk and crawling over the flower. The position of the floral parts has to be appropriate or pollination would not be effected. The American bat collects most of its pollen on the back of the neck and head, so that is the site where the female flower parts have to touch at the bat's next visit. On the Old World bat the pollen is picked up on the belly.

A problem over which plants have little control is the attacks of nectar-robbers. These animals, usually large bees or bats, attack the flower just before it has opened by cutting a hole in the back and stealing the nectar without effecting pollination.

Not all animals that visit flowers seek nectar. Bees collect pollen in order to make the "bee bread" with which they feed their brood. Long-lived butterflies, such as *Heliconius,* would be unable to maintain their egg production over a three-month period if they were not able to supplement their supply of nitrogen by digesting pollen externally with stomach enzymes and then sucking up the slurry through their proboscis.

There are some remarkable cases in which the animal visitor seeks neither nectar nor pollen. The American euglossine bees are such a case. The females emerge from their parental cell and forage for nectar and pollen in an opportunistically and typically beelike manner. The males,

Above. *The emergent crowns of some tropical forest trees are often aflame with blossom during periods of leaflessness. These flowers of an* Erythrina *from Brazil give some feeling for the intensity of the displays.*

Opposite. *The fruits of* Blighia sapida *were carried by slaves from its native West Africa to Jamaica late in the eighteenth century. It is the creamy-white aril of the slave fruit, or akee, which partially surrounds the black seeds and is eaten either raw or cooked. Great care is needed in the preparation of the food—the pink raphe by which the seed and aril are connected and the unripe arils are highly poisonous and can prove fatal if consumed. The genus was named after Captain Bligh of H.M.S.* Bounty.

however, are vagabonds and roam far and wide in search of fragrant orchids. When they find a suitable species they climb inside the flower, scrape the petals with their front legs, and detach some of the material responsible for the fragrance. This material they pack into a pouch on their hind legs. When the collection is built up to an adequate level the males fly in open areas and attract other males by their aroma. There may be fifty or sixty males congregating together, attracted by each other's scent, and it is into these swarms that the virgin females fly. Soon after they enter the swarm, they are seized by a male and taken off to be mated. This specialized behavior of the males has many similarities to the courtship of some bird species which are individually widely dispersed during the nonbreeding season. Lastly, there is the ultimate in deception. There are orchids that bear a remarkable resemblance to female bees. Naive males, which emerge from their pupal cells before their females, are deceived, enter the flower, and attempt to copulate. In the process they become dusted with pollen which they then transfer to the next case of mistaken identity.

Thus, we see that the relationships between plants and their pollinators are intricate. Any disturbance of the forest can throw the system off balance and have far-reaching effects. But the pollinated flower has only just begun to fulfill its primary biological function, that of reproduction. The plant still has to set seeds and arrange for them to be dispersed.

Above. (both) *A botanist, not an entomologist, would collect this specimen of* Pleurothallis raymondii, *an orchid from Venezuela. Most flowers offer only nectar as a reward for flower visitation by potential pollinators, but orchids are unique. Many species offer perfume, which is collected by male euglossine bees, while others simulate female insects and deceive naive males into attempted copulation. Although the male receives no gratification from these encounters, the insect unwittingly transfers pollen from one flower to another.*

Above. *The orchid* Lepanthes calodictyon *from Colombia has a flower that resembles a fly or other small insect. Real insects are attracted to the mimic and incidentally serve as pollinators. There is no known trapping of the insect visitors involved, for they must be allowed to escape or they would be unable to transfer pollen from one flower to another. This is a cheap system, for the flower wastes no energy in manufacturing nectar.*

Left. Dendrobium veratrifolium *from New Guinea might be called the "rabbit ears" orchid, for each flower has a pair of erect earlike petals. The orchids are so resplendent that it is no surprise that they have been a focus for horticulturists for more than a thousand years.*

Opposite. *The croton is a popular ornamental plant, native to the rain forests of Malaya, and has been cultivated for many years. Breeders and selectors have isolated this "tortilis" cultivar of* Codiaeum variegatus *because of its twisted and variegated leaves. The wild ancestor has the same variegations but has flat leaves.*

Left. Lobelia centrophogen *from Tingo María, Peru, is reminiscent of the heads of the flamingos used as croquet mallets in Lewis Carroll's* Alice's Adventures in Wonderland. *All they lack is an eye!*

Below. *Popular as a cultivated temperate houseplant,* Aphelandra squarrosa, *or zebra plant, is native to Brazilian rain forests but is now rare in the wild.*

Following pages. *Flowers that are pollinated by moths, such as this striking* Epidendrum cilare *from Panama, are frequently white or cream, and are open or fragrant only during the evening hours when the pollinator is on the wing. The odor of moth-pollinated flowers is usually reminiscent of vegetables, rather than fruits.*

Right. *At the marginal rain-forest altitudes in Sri Lanka, one of the beautiful flowers is that of* Osbeckia cupularis.

Center. *The sensitive plant,* Mimosa pudica, *is a native to Brazil but is now widely distributed throughout the tropics. The ability of the leaves to fold up when touched has been the subject of many perplexing scientific investigations. The function of the leaf movement, which reduces the surface area when wet, is thought to lower heat loss through surface evaporation. The first few drops of rain cause the leaflets to fold up, presenting a very small target.*

Bottom. *Only the down feathers of a hatchling bird can match the exquisite elegance of the flower of* Cyanotis pilosa *from Sri Lanka.*

Above. (right & left) *This most unusual flower from Bahia, Brazil, is that of* Spathicarpa sagittifolia.

Left. *The Philippine jade vine* (Strongylodon macrobotrys) *is most unusual in having blue-green flowers. There can be no doubt that birds potentially act as pollinators, for here is one caught in the act of visiting.*

Above. (left) Bulbophyllum medusae *(Orchidaceae) is a remarkable orchid with sepals lengthened into six-inch-long (15 cm) yellow threads dotted with red. It is a native of Malaya, Borneo, and some East Indian islands.*

(right) *The pouch orchids, such as this* Phragmipedium caudatum *from Peru, are reminiscent of the insectivorous pitcher plants, but the specialized structure is directed only at ensuring pollination. Many of the pouch or bucket orchids have a device whereby bees and other insects that visit the flower fall into the bucket and are allowed to escape only via a special tunnel. During their passage through the tunnel they donate and pick up pollen, which is carried to the next bucket orchid they visit. This is a seemingly complex method of ensuring pollination, but it must be efficient or the orchids would not have survived.*

Opposite. Paphiopedilium venustum *is a Himalayan orchid that is allegedly nearing extinction. Flies are the probable pollinators, for the flowers typically smell fetid.*

Left. *The elegant* Doritis pulcherrima *orchid from Thailand is most likely pollinated by large bees (Xylocopidae).*

Above. *Not all orchids are large and showy. This tiny* Podochilus lucescens *from Sumatra is mature and in full bloom and yet is smaller than a Singapore twenty-cent piece.*

Above. (right) *This diminutive high-altitude orchid,* Masdevallia, *is from Colombia at nine thousand feet (2,750 m) and has most delicate threadlike petals.*

Right. *The ancestors of the cultivated* Miltonia *orchid were natives of Colombia and Panama. Known as Meadowdale Robin Hood, this spectacular flower is a good example of the orchid breeder's art. New tissue culture techniques enable breeders to grow complete plants from single cells. From each cell a complete plant that is an exact copy of the parent can be developed. This cloning technique ensures the duplicity of the desired features of the original parent and has revolutionized orchid growing. Similar success is now being realized with agricultural crop varieties but, as yet, no success has been recorded in mammals—most particularly, humans.*

Animals in a Perpetual High

TINSTAAFL—There Is No Such Thing As A Free Lunch has become a familiar complaint in our modern welfare society, but for many of the rain-forest animals the fruit that ripens on the rain-forest trees is truly free. The fleshy fruit is originally intended for dispersal agents that will release the contained seeds at a distant site, perhaps to germinate and mature. However, there are legions of animals, both within and beneath the canopy, that prey upon the fruit and seeds and provide nothing in return. Forest trees have had to develop strategies against these freeloaders or their species would not have survived.

Trees and lianas in the upper levels of the forest canopy are the only plant freeloaders, for they can depend on wind for the dispersal of their seeds, but the wind is only really trustworthy in the drier seasons. Thomas Croat has shown that in Panama 97 percent of the epiphytes that flower in the dry season have wind-dispersed seeds, whereas of those that flower in the wet season the percentage is only 23. Wind dispersal can be very effective, for there are authentic records of fern spores being wind-dispersed to oceanic islands over distances of two thousand miles (1,240 km). Wind dispersal has its price, for the seeds have to be light, and that means they cannot contain very much food reserve. Most rain-forest plants need substantial food reserves in their seeds in order for their seedlings to compete effectively in the race for light. Thus, we find that most trees have specialized in relatively large seeds that employ birds, mammals, and occasionally fish for their dispersal. The most common strategy is for the tree to develop highly visible fruits of striking color with a tasty flesh and poisonous seeds. The bribe offered is usually in the form of sugar, which the plant can well afford to give away, hence the flesh of the fruit is usually poor in proteins and fats. The more precious nutrients are invested in the seeds, for those reserves are the sole resources of the seedling until it has become established and can photosynthesize for itself. The dispersal agent, usually a bird, bat, or arboreal mammal, picks the fruit and either drops the seeds after eating the flesh or passes the swallowed but unmasticated and undigested seeds out with its feces. This latter ploy has the special advantage that the disperser will most likely be far from the parent tree when it defecates the seeds. However, the seed has to avoid being destroyed in the animal's gut and it must be unpalatable to the disperser, hence it requires a special seed coat and an investment of distasteful poisons. Some seeds actually require that they be exposed to the digestive enzymes of their disperser's gut in order to be capable of germinating.

The most effective dispersal agents are birds, such as toucans (*Rhamphastos*), which are strong fliers and are exclusively fruit eaters, for they are wide ranging and frequently drop their seeds in flight. The more opportunistic fruit eaters, such as flycatchers (*Myiozetetes*), have such a wide variety of foods that they tend to be more restricted in their flight range and are therefore weaker dispersal agents.

Just as the trees have temporally separated flowering

patterns that supply their pollinators with nectar all year round, so fruiting is spaced out to benefit dispersers. In Trinidad nineteen species of *Miconia* (Melastomaceae) fruit appear sequentially throughout the year, a strategy that reduces competition for dispersers between the species and keeps the animals alive with a regular supply of food. However, continuous fruit fall can be hazardous, for if there are few other sources of food available, populations of seed predators can build up to levels that may destroy the seed crop as fast as it is produced. The Dipterocarpaceae, a group of trees in Southeast Asia, have highly edible seeds that would be continuously devoured by predators if they were released gradually. Instead, the individuals of a particular species of tree produce no fruit for five to twenty-one years and then, in response to a single environmental cue, over an area of hundreds of square kilometers, they all flower and fruit together. The principle seems to be that by holding back their fruiting for a long period, they starve out their local seed predators and satiate the survivors with a massive fruit drop at long intervals.

There is continuous cooperation between the trees and their dispersal agents. Costa Rica has the highest density of bird species in the world, with 758 species over an area of 21,000 square miles (55,000 km²). It is not coincidence that, at 90 percent, the proportion of trees that produce fleshy fruit is also one of the highest. Only 10 percent of the tree species in Sarawak produce fleshy fruits and the bird population of that country is far below the 356 known from the whole of Malaya's 83,000 square miles (215,000 km²).

Ornithologists who arise with the dawn and immediately clamp a spotting 'scope to their orbits may be disappointed with the cursory treatment of rain-forest birds. The phrase "as scarce as hen's teeth" is an avian truism, for it is one hundred million years since an ancestor of modern birds was known to possess teeth and typifies the extreme uniformity of bird anatomy. However, one cannot apply the paraphrased words of Ronald Reagan, lately Governor of California, "when you have seen one [bird] you have seen them all," for although the demands of aviation have imposed severe constraints on bone structure, birds exhibit an extraordinary diversity of behavior, plumage, and ecological role.

The rain forest offers more ecological niches than any other ecosystem and birds have exploited them all. There are birds which are characteristic of each canopy layer and there are even flightless birds, such as the tinamou of South America which is confined to the forest floor. The density of bird species reaches its maximum in the rain forest and peaks in South America. Almost all the spectacular birds that fascinate visitors of the tropical-bird house in zoological gardens are rain-forest inhabitants.

Rain-forest birds feed on nectar, fruit, seeds, insects, and mammals up to the size of monkeys. They play an important role in the recycling of nutrients, in the dispersal of seeds, and in the regulation of insect populations. Some birds are specialists, such as the South American antbirds,

Preceding pages. (left) *Howler monkeys (*Alouatta *sp.) are tropical American treetop dwellers which live in family groups of five to thirty individuals, including infants. Although frequently nocturnal, these monkeys are most active in the morning and late afternoon, when they forage for young leaves, fruit, seeds, small animals, and bird eggs. Only the males "howl," or rather roar, and over lakes their sounds can be heard at least two miles. Unlike most other rain-forest mammals in Central America, the numbers of howler monkeys seem to be increasing, perhaps because they favor secondary forest and disturbed habitats.*

(right) *The three-toed sloth (*Bradypus tridactylus) *is an important rain-forest-canopy herbivore. It has been estimated that in both Surinam and on Barro Colorado Island in Panama the diurnal sloth (*Bradypus) *is the most abundant mammal, and together with its nocturnal relative* Choloepus *(the two-toed sloth) they comprise 20 and 50 percent respectively of the total mammal biomass. They spend almost all their time in the treetops, so they are easily overlooked.*

Above. *Monkeys in South America have developed independently of those from Asia and Africa, for the continents have been separated for about eighty-five million years. South American monkeys can be distinguished by their prehensile tails and more numerous teeth. There are many unsolved problems concerning the origin of the New World monkeys, for the fossil record is embarrassingly incomplete. Illustrated is* Saimiri scuireus, *the squirrel monkey from Peru, which lives gregariously in the forest canopy throughout South America and feeds on lizards, eggs, and insects.*

Right. *There are only four characteristically different types of living ape: the chimpanzee and gorilla of Africa, and the gibbon and orangutan of Southeast Asia and Indonesia. In the reserves of Sandakan in Sabah, where this orangutan lives, their numbers are counted now in the low thousands. One wonders how much longer they will survive in the wild with their habitat rapidly being destroyed. Fifty years? Twenty-five years? Less?*

Above. *The name* Pithecophaga jefferyi *was well chosen, for it literally means "monkey-eating." These eagles are among the most powerful birds of prey and subsist principally on macaques that live in their native Philippines. Other than the identity of their prey, little is known of the biology of these impressive birds, less than one hundred of which remain in the wild.*

which feed exclusively on army ants, while others feed on both nectar and insects as they are available.

Temperate-zone ornithologists would recognize the families of many rain-forest birds, for they have representatives in northern climates; such familiar animals include hummingbirds, flycatchers, owls, hawks, and woodpeckers. But many families are exclusively tropical and would be identified only by the educated observer. The more flamboyant species are illustrated in every nature encyclopedia and include parrots, parakeets, hornbills, toucans, birds-of-paradise, and myna birds. The domesticated chicken is a descendant of the red jungle fowl from Southeast Asian rain forests.

The extreme density of the rain-forest foliage makes flight difficult within the canopy. Most herbivorous birds are much more adept at walking along tree branches than are their temperate relatives. Only predatory birds that hunt over the top of the forest and hummingbirds, which feed while hovering, are in flight for long periods of time.

The diversity of the rain forest enables predators to specialize as well as prey, so some birds have adopted extreme measures to secure their brood. Some hornbills, for example, wall themselves into a hollow tree by plastering over the entrance, leaving a hole only large enough for the male outside to pass in food for his mate and her developing brood. Only when the fledglings are mature does the female burst the wall of their prison and set them free.

Our knowledge of the mammals that inhabit the rain-forest canopy is scanty. It is true we know of the larger mammals, such as the anteaters (*Tamandua, Cyclopes*), sloths (*Bradypus, Choloepus*), opossums (*Didelphis*), porcupines (*Coendou*), and monkeys and marmosets of South and Central America; the pangolins (*Manis*), tree hydraxes (*Dendrohyrax*), porcupines (*Atherurus*), and monkeys and apes of Africa and Southeast Asia, but the biology of very few of these animals is known with confidence. Zoo studies reveal little of the habits of the animals in the wild, although in many cases they provide the only information we can glean. The greatest handicap to behavioral studies of these animals is the inaccessibility of the canopy and the formidable lengths of time that effective studies demand. Jane Lawick-Goodall, of chimpanzee-work fame, has estimated that five hundred hours is the minimum time required in the field to obtain basic understanding of the habits of apes. She spent more than fifteen hundred hours making her landmark observations of the chimpanzees of Gombe Reserve in Tanzania.

Perhaps it is unfair to select ape behavior as a standard for mammalian field studies, for recent work on chimpanzees, orangutans, and gorillas has shown them to be inordinately complex and flexible animals. Chimpanzees are now known to have regional dialects in gesticulations and grooming behavior; thus it will be impossible at any point in the near future to place a checkmark against chimpanzee and say that it has been "done." There are, instead, levels of

Above. *Oilbirds* (Steatornis caripensis) *are so-called for the extraordinary fat content of the fledglings, which weigh as much as 150 percent of the weight of the adult bird. South American Indians used oilbird fat as a source of heat for cooking and for light. Oilbirds navigate at night by making audible clicks and interpreting the echoes from the environment in the manner of bats. The most accessible colony is in the Arima Valley in Trinidad, although additional colonies are known in other localities in northern South America. The birds are also known as* guacharos, *which in Spanish means "one who cries and laments," presumably because of their garrulous squawking when disturbed.*

study beyond which the law of diminishing returns argues against further investment of time and money. It seems likely that this point has been approached in the case of field observations on the chimpanzee and gorilla, for our knowledge of the orangutan, siamang, and gibbon is much weaker. Yet in 1978 laboratory chimpanzees were found to be using a newly learned human sign language for communicating with each other, so perhaps a whole new area of inquiry is opening.

The studies of Sherwood Washburn and Irven DeVore in the early 1960s showed that baboons, which are plains-dwelling monkeys, had a strict, hierarchical social structure with a dominant male as a leader and a descending order of subordinate males and females. These findings were used for many years as a benchmark for comparisons with the behavior of other primates and became regarded as typical of baboons in general. However, later studies by Thelma Rowell have shown that in areas where food resources were much more abundant than in the localities studied by Washburn and DeVore, the social structure was much less rigid and the females played a more important role in leadership. A biological truth which has been forced on modern behaviorists is that generalizations cannot be founded with confidence on studies of a single population of animals.

There seem to be basic differences between the social organization of plains-dwelling monkeys, such as the baboon and the macaque, and their forest counterparts. The canopy foliage presents such a safe and bountiful environment for mobile animals that they can afford to have a loosely knit social structure that allows great freedom to the individual. It is no coincidence that such a habitat spawned the development of apes whose intelligence is second only to that of humans.

The protection of the rain-forest canopy has enabled some of its animals to form long-term teaching associations with their infants. The newborn chimpanzee enjoys about four years of maternal care before it becomes potentially independent. There would be no such opportunity on the plains, for there an animal must be born in such a condition that it can run within minutes, or fall as prey to a predator. The newborn ape is helpless and totally dependent on its mother for food, protection, and transport.

In the case of the apes, sheer bulk confers an additional protective advantage, for there are few predators able to tackle an adult chimpanzee, and none the equal of a gorilla. Size has its handicaps, however, for the weight of the gorilla limits the trees it can utilize and so they spend much of their time on the ground. The smaller animals, such as monkeys and gibbons, are almost totally arboreal and rarely descend to the forest floor unless exploiting unusually rich fruit resources.

No predator, other than a speeding bullet, can catch a monkey fleeing through the canopy. Donald Perry has shown that the canopy has a network of arboreal highways kept open by habitual use. Epiphytes continue to grow on

Opposite. *Together with hummingbirds, toucans and macaws are the birds most closely associated with tropical America. Popular at zoos and as pets, the macaws are now being overexploited and are threatened with extinction. These brilliant birds are scarlet macaws* (Ara maceo) *from Brazil.*

Above. *The New World has toucans, the Old World has hornbills. All hornbills mate for life and most have a most peculiar method of raising their young. The male cements the mated female into a hollow tree with clay until only the tip of her bill is exposed. He then feeds her, and later her chicks, through the entrance hole. Only when the chicks are half-grown is the female allowed to emerge and assist in foraging for food for the brood. The thickening on the top of the bill is hollow in some species and solid in others. The bills of those species in which the swelling is solid are highly prized for ivory carving. This specimen of* Rhyncoceres cassodix *is in a zoo where it will probably outlive its wild relatives.*

Above. *Hummingbirds are a characteristic feature of the warmer regions of the Americas, where they pollinate many flower species. This unidentified hummingbird is from Ecuador.*

the sides of the highway branches but are removed or trodden underfoot along the tops. It has been estimated that before the cutting of the trans-Amazonian highway, a monkey could have traveled from Colombia to Argentina without ever touching the ground!

Our knowledge of the fauna of the rain-forest canopy is in its infancy, yet we seem destined to remain forever ignorant, for it seems doubtful that many significant advances will be made before the forests are destroyed. Such projections render academic the problems of listing species as endangered and seeking legislation to protect them. We can be appalled at the traffic in tropical birds and monkeys out of the rain forest, and indeed it is atrocious, but the long-term policing of the forest reserves is of doubtful viability. The flow of stomach-turning stories of animal captures and transport seems impossible to stop. Currently, we hear of the execution of a family of mountain gorillas in Tanzania, done either in revenge for the establishment of a game reserve or to provide trophies. We learn of poachers leaving unwanted birds to die in traps to avoid the inconvenience of catching them twice. How can such brutality be controlled? The United States government has taken beneficial action in refusing an import license for any animal protected in its country of origin. Yet the Rajah Brooke's birdwing and other endangered tropical butterflies are still for sale in our naturalists' collector stores! They are poached. Protection is beneficial only when it can be enforced effectively, which is rarely the case. Listing a species as endangered pushes up the price and makes extensive poaching economical.

Perhaps because we can see ourselves mirrored in their faces, the chimpanzees have earned a special place in our hearts. It seems likely that they will pay dearly for the resemblance, for not only are they physically comparable to humans, but they are also immunologically similar. A human vaccine for hepatitis B virus has been developed but requires the importation of a relatively large number of chimpanzees. A request has been made by a pharmaceutical company to the United States Fish and Wildlife Service for permission to import 125 animals, a seemingly modest number. However, the most popular method of capture is to shoot the mother and capture the infant. It has been estimated that six hundred chimpanzees will be killed to satisfy the delivery order. The wild populations of chimpanzees cannot withstand such attrition in addition to the pressures they already experience. Which is more important, an animal or a human? Animals are now in conflict with human needs. We are in competition with the canopy dwellers for land, food, and the very right to life. Peter Singer has summed it up well in his book *Animal Liberation: A New Ethic for Our Treatment of Animals.* We hold ourselves in such high esteem that we ride roughshod over all other organisms. Perhaps one day we will meet Sir Charles Kingsley's character from *The Water Babies* whose name, I recall, was "Be-done-by-as-you-did."

Above. The hummingbirds are the smallest birds known and are confined to the Americas. They all feed while hovering on nectar or nectar and insects. In flight, their wingbeats can exceed eighty per second. Males are usually more highly decorated than females. This illustration is of Anna's hummingbird (Calypte anna) from western California, where it remains a year-round resident. Ornithologists are puzzled by the ability of these small birds to fly long distances during migrations. The rapid wingbeats consume so much energy that it seems doubtful that sufficient fuel can be carried. Do they ride on the backs of other birds? We await the first such sighting with excitement!

The Night Club

Anthropomorphism, or ascribing human perceptions and qualities to nonhuman things, such as animals, is a pleasurable, scientific sin. Those of us who are dog lovers frequently imagine that we can climb inside our animated teddy bear's skin and look out at the world through its soft brown eyes. Of course, in our more critical moments we accept that we have no real conception of the world in which our pets live, for our only experiences are as witnessed through human sensitivity. Hidebound by the limitation of our own senses, it is not surprising that we have such difficulty understanding a bird's ability to navigate by using the earth's magnetic field or a male moth's ability to detect a female from a distance of sixteen miles (26 km).

Anthropologists believe that humans have had a long history of hunting game and gathering fruits, foliage, and roots on the plains of Africa. We are certainly equipped to fit the role, for we are diurnal and visually oriented. How different we are from the nocturnal animals of the forest which confine their activities to the hours between dusk and dawn. Theirs is a world of sound, odor, and warmth. Our senses do not even match those of the diurnal rain-forest animals, for in the windless forest interior, smell and sight are so unreliable that only communication by sound is feasible.

If we are alert, we can detect the heat radiated from a hot saucepan just in time to avoid picking it up. What would it feel like to detect the warmth of a mouse from two or three meters? Pit vipers, boid snakes, and owls can do it! We boast that we have exceptional vision, but it is really only our color vision that is noteworthy. If a falcon were able to read, it could read a newspaper from a hundred meters! These levels of perception are so far beyond our comprehension that in the investigation of animal senses we have to throw away our human-oriented standards and depend on instruments and logic.

Standing still in a rain-forest clearing just after dusk, you will perceive a cacophony of sound beyond the buzzing of the mosquito in your ear. While the diurnal vocalists, such as monkeys, apes, grasshoppers, cicadas, and birds, are silently sleeping, their place has been taken by frogs, toads, crickets, and katydids. Once again we have been deceived by the inadequacies of our senses for we have overlooked the bats, the most vocal of all the nocturnal animals. Although bats make some audible squeaks, the vast majority of their sounds are emitted at frequencies far above our range of hearing. As babies we may be able to detect frequencies as high as twenty thousand cycles per second, usually written 20 kilohertz (kHz), but as we age, the inner and middle ear become less responsive so that by the time we are middle aged we are probably limited to 16 kHz, and by retirement the threshold has fallen to nearer 14 kHz. Dogs have good hearing up to about 22 kHz, an ability which is exploited in the use of humanly inaudible training whistles. Such sounds that are above the threshold of human perception are termed ultrasonic.

Insectivorous bats navigate and locate their prey by

analyzing the echoes of ultrasonic sounds emitted while in flight. The echolocation system is known as sonar. With experience, bats learn the patterns of reflection from their hunting territories and fly in the dark with the confidence of a bird in daylight. Although zoologists have known for many years that bats are not really blind, Donald Griffin and some of his graduate students at the Rockefeller Institute for Research in Animal Behavior became interested in the extent to which bats really depend on vision in their nocturnal hunting forays. In order to test their visual capability, a large number of bats were collected from a cave roost near the William Beebe Tropical Research Station in Trinidad and divided into three groups of equal size, which we will call A, B, and C. Group A served as the control and the bats were not altered in any way other than to mark them with paint so that they could be distinguished from bats not involved in the experiment. The bats in Group B had a pair of lensless spectacles cemented to their face, which as far as could be determined did not impair their vision. The bats in Group C had spectacles cemented to their faces in the same manner as those of Group B, but the rims were fitted with opaque lenses that rendered the bats totally blind.

The experimental bats were taken by automobile during the late afternoon toward the flat farmland to the south of the foothills of the Northern Range. At different distances from their home cave, samples of the bats were daubed with identifying paint and released, ensuring that at each release site an equal number of groups A, B, and C were liberated. Over the next few weeks, the cave was thoroughly collected every day for the returning bats. The final data showed that the bats released within their home valley all found their way back regardless of whether they were blind or not. As the distance from the cave increased, the proportion of returning blind bats gradually decreased when compared with that of bats with unimpaired vision. The lack of difference between the returns of those bats with lensless spectacles and those with no spectacles at all indicated that the novel presence of the rims alone appeared to have no effect on their performance. However, from beyond a critical distance very few of the bats returned, whether spectacled, blind, or unmodified. A few stragglers returned over the next few months, but most of the bats were never seen again. Clearly, beyond a certain distance away from the mountains the bats were unable to find their way home.

In a seemingly unrelated experiment, Roderick Suthers then tested the ability of the bats to discriminate between black and white lines of varying width. Individually, unmodified bats were allowed to hang from a stationary perch inside a large revolving drum, the interior of which was lined with replaceable paper. Initially the paper was painted with broad black-and-white vertical stripes of even widths. When the drum began to revolve, the hanging bat turned its head as it watched the stripes change position, indicating that the bat must have been able to distinguish the individual stripes. The experiment was repeated with

narrower and narrower stripes, until a stripe width was reached at which the bat no longer turned its head when the drum began to revolve. At that stripe width, we presume the bat saw only a uniform gray background and was unable to distinguish the stripes individually. It is surely no coincidence that the angle between the eyes of the bat and the edges of the stripes that the bat could not see was the same as the angle between the top of the home-range mountains and the plains horizon at the release point beyond which the bats could not find their way home! It would seem that these bats used their echolocating system in familiar surroundings near their home roost, but used vision for the identification of landmarks when far away. The adage "as blind as a bat" seems far from being apt.

In the mid-1960s, the United States Navy became interested in the fish-eating noctilionid bats that hunt in the sea off the coast of Baja California and northeastern South America. The Navy's question was "Can a fish-eating bat detect a fish that is totally submerged?" for if bats can do it, then perhaps a machine could be invented that could detect the presence of submarines from the air. Experiments with simulated prey in a flight-cage pond showed that if as little as a cubic millimeter of prey appeared above the water surface, the bats would notice it and strike with their long claws, but if the prey was totally submerged the bats were completely unaware of its presence. The Navy has lost interest in bats!

The bat fauna of the tropics is vast. Species lists of mammals grow rapidly as one travels from temperate to tropical latitudes, but the increase is attributable entirely to increasing numbers of bats, for the number of species of nonbat mammals actually declines. The warm, moist tropical rain forests are ideal bat environments, for the great energy demands of flight require that the animals maintain a high body temperature in spite of having a potentially large rate of heat loss from the extensive wing area. The roofs of caves provide excellent protection from predators during the day, their relatively low temperatures being offset by communal roosting. The ceilings of bat caves are covered from wall to wall with tightly packed bats. If you approach they drop off the ceiling and fly toward the entrance, but as they attempt to avoid you, and each other, it is inevitable that they caress you with their cool, velvety wings—not really unpleasant at all.

There are two basic kinds of bat: the Microchiroptera, which are worldwide in distribution but concentrated in the Americas, and the Megachiroptera, which are confined to the Old World of Africa and Asia. The Microchiroptera are generally predatory, feeding on insects, birds, fish, other bats, and the blood of larger mammals, although many species also eat fruit and nectar and may play an important part in the pollination and seed dispersal of rain-forest trees. In Costa Rica, Daniel Janzen found an estimated fifty-five thousand seeds of *Piper auritum* beneath a fruit-eating bat's feeding roost, which may explain why these plants sometimes grow in dense clumps.

The Megachiroptera are fruit and nectar feeders and are only occasionally involved in predation. The enormous fifty-inch (1.3-m) wingspan of *Pteropus giganteus* justifies their being known as flying foxes. They roost communally in trees in groups of up to a thousand, and many visitors to the tropics have been kept awake at night by their incessant chattering after a foraging expedition. Bats may travel up to thirty miles (50 km) during a foraging trip. These fruit-eating bats do not have their echolocating system nearly as well developed as that of the insectivorous bats, and they depend much more on their sense of smell in the location of their food.

The Microchiroptera, on the other hand, have a highly developed echolocating system. During an attempt at prey capture, an insectivorous bat emits a series of ultrasonic signals ranging between 50 and 100 kHz, according to the individual species. The scientific investigator is armed with a "bat detector," which is an instrument that translates inaudible high-frequency sounds into audible sounds of similar duration. If the highly direction-sensitive microphone of the detector is pointed toward a cruising bat, a series of clicks about one tenth of a second apart will be emitted from the bat and heard over the speaker. When the bat hears the echo of its sounds reflected from an unfamiliar object, such as an insect in the air, it accelerates its rate of click production to about thirty per second and focuses directly on the target. If the echo reinforces the identification of the object as a potential prey, the bat spreads its feet (and tail fan if it has one), accelerates its pulse rate up to as much as two hundred per second, and sweeps the insect into its mouth. Bats with storage pouches in their cheeks have been known to catch five hundred insects in an hour.

Among the more notable tropical-forest bats are the vampires of Central and South America. These unexpectedly small bats lap the blood that wells up from the neck or shoulder wounds they inflict on large sleeping mammals with their razor-sharp incisors. The blood is prevented from clotting by an anticoagulant in the bat's saliva, but the amount of pain inflicted by the bite is dependent only on the skill of the bat. Young inexperienced bats frequently arouse their victim by their crude surgery. The great false vampire (*Vampyrum spectrum*), one of the largest bats in South America, with a wingspan of nearly thirty inches (.76 cm), is a voracious hunter of small mammals, which it kills instantly by crushing their skulls with its teeth!

Bats are such skilled predators that their potential prey go to great lengths to avoid being caught. If a flying noctuid moth hears the accelerating pulses of an attacking bat, it performs violent aerobatics, closes its wings, and drops to the ground, an avoiding reaction that frequently allows it to escape. Arctiid moths, which are thought to be distasteful to bats or other predators, exhibit a more sophisticated defense. These moths have both a hearing organ and a sound-producing organ. The sound is produced by

Above. *Fruit bats roost communally in trees by day; almost all are nocturnal. Their short jaws and powerful teeth allow them to pierce the rinds of tough fruit.*

"popping" a cymbal-like patch of cuticle in and out. The cymbal bears a row of dimples of increasing size, so that when the cymbal is popped each dimple pops as well, creating a zipping sound over a wide range of ultrasonic frequencies. When the flying moth hears the signals of an oncoming bat, it rapidly pops the cymbal in and out. If the bat that hears the zips has already learned from a previous encounter that these moths have a disagreeable taste, it will veer away and make no further attempt to catch it.

One of the attractive aspects of bat research is the opportunity of using ingenious equipment and techniques. In the field, bats are caught in fine mist nets, tracked with glued-on light tags and radio transmitters, listened to with bat detectors, and recorded with ultrasonic tape recorders. The recordings are analyzed for pitch, intensity, and duration with a sound analyzer. All heady stuff for the electronics enthusiast.

During the mid-1960s to 1970s, it was inevitable that bat researchers were nicknamed Batman by their students. Of all my experiences with Batmen, there is one that I will not easily forget. I was showing off the zoological delights of Trinidad to Theresa Clay, a British Museum specialist in mammal parasites. We had planned a visit to Tamana caves in the Central Range of the island, where there is a colony of many thousands of bats in a fairly accessible cave. It turned out that the local Batman was also visiting the caves, with a Canadian mammalogist and other interested visitors. He invited us to join his party, which we were pleased to do, but from the first greeting, early that morning, we got off to a bad start. "Good to have you along, boy," said Batman in a southern United States drawl. But it was my eyes that I could not believe, not my ears. Batman was dressed in black leather snake boots which almost reached his thighs, an Australian-type bush jacket, and a ten-gallon hat. Projecting across his ample belly were a pair of pearl-handled revolvers. His reason for having the handles facing each other was, apparently, because he could "draw" faster with them that way around. Laughing into our hands, we set off for the cave. Theresa and I were dressed in the traditional tropical three S's—shirt, shorts, and sneakers. Our collecting kit consisted of a rope to lower ourselves into the cave, a headlight apiece, a cardboard box with a flap in the top, gloves, and a butterfly net.

When we reached the cave, we set a good example and belayed our rope, lowered ourselves into the cave, and set about catching bats with our butterfly net. The atmosphere in the cave was as damp as expected from the urine raining down from the bats roosting on the ceiling and the ground was spongy with decomposing fruit and seeds. Many seeds had germinated, but in the absence of light they had no chance of further growth. We were somewhat surprised that none of the other people had followed us into the cave, but we could hear the pop-pop of the six-shooters beyond the cave entrance, so we knew that they had not left. When we had caught about fifty bats and scraped some parasitic streblid fly-cases off the walls, we returned into the daylight. To our amazement, none of the ten-strong party had dared to enter the cave, and the only bat that had been caught was hit in flight with a stick wielded by a visiting Norwegian seaman! We felt quite smug when we offered to share our catch, and self-righteous when they accepted.

When collecting in the forest, choice of dress is important, and our wearing sneakers was rather foolish, for both the bushmaster (*Lachesis muta*) and the fer-de-lance (*Bothrops atrox*) were common. However, both these snakes are nocturnal, so the chances of meeting them were slim unless we were careless. At night the situation would have been different. A good maxim is "Never place your foot where you have not already cast your eye!" The bites of large venomous snakes are very dangerous even with speedy and appropriate medical treatment, which is rarely available in the forest. The record size for the bushmaster is eleven feet, four inches (3.35 m), measured from a specimen from Costa Rica with fangs an inch and a quarter (30 mm) long!

Fortunately, snakes detect the approach of human footsteps from a considerable distance and usually glide quietly away. Stories of the American bushmaster chasing people are quite unfounded. The larger vipers are usually sluggish and are aggressive only when threatened. One reason for the slow movement of ground-dwelling nocturnal snakes is the relatively cool temperatures. For many years the curators of North American and European zoos were unable to keep the bushmaster in captivity, for the snakes would not take food and had difficulty shedding their skins. Then it was realized that the tropical reptile house, with its 77°F (25°C) temperature, was much too hot. When the cage was kept at about 66°F (19°C), the snakes thrived and even reproduced. On several occasions, I recorded temperatures of less than 59°F (15°C) on the forest floor in Trinidad in the early morning. During my professional life in Trinidad, when I latterly became involved in studying katydids, snakes became a waning interest, revived only when I visited the insect traps at night.

Nocturnal insects use two types of communication that we can readily recognize: sound and light. Male katydids and crickets are familiar singers in temperate climates; in the tropics their numbers are multiplied a hundredfold. The evening air is filled with such a symphony of sound that one wonders how the females can distinguish the songs of their own males from all the others. While collecting insects at night and listening to their songs, one cannot avoid seeing the flashing lights of the fireflies (which are really beetles).

In Southeast Asia, generations of male fireflies collect on particular trees on the riverbanks and display uninterruptedly for years. Native boatmen learn to use the trees as navigational beacons. The flashing of the males is inhibited by bright light, even their own, so unable to be close to each other they are widely dispersed throughout the canopies. Females enter the flashing area, return the flashes, and select a mate. Each species has a different

Opposite. Some water lilies are members of the night club, for their flowers bloom only at night. Many gardeners have been highly disappointed in never seeing their nocturnal lilies bloom. Night-opening lilies are naturally pollinated by moths or bats. Water lilies are elegant aquatic ornamentals and are widely distributed in the tropics. Many new varieties of species of Nymphaea *(Nymphaeaceae) have been bred. Blue star is illustrated here.*

Opposite. (top) Pycnopalpa, *nocturnal katydids (Tettigoniidae) from South America, are among the most beautifully camouflaged of all insects. Although the overall insect shape is retained, the leaflike wings have simulated necrotic spots on them. Notice particularly how, in the normal resting position, the hind leg is colored brown where it overlaps the brown pattern on the body and wings. The pattern is genetically fixed; long series of specimens show very little variation.*

(bottom) *Being exclusively nocturnal,* Paraphidnia *katydids have to have excellent camouflage during the day. This specimen from Manaus, Amazonas, blends very well with its background— provided it keeps still. Notice how irregular the antennae are, a feature of* Paraphidnia.

flashing rate—some flash every half second, some every second, and some only once every three seconds. Yet, all the males of one species flash in unison, perhaps to make it harder for a predator to concentrate on a single individual.

A firefly story with a twist to it has been told by James Lloyd. He reports that some predatory females have a repertoire of several flashing patterns in addition to that of their own species. Sitting in the trees, they flash the sexual signal of a foreign species and lure the males into their waiting arms—and jaws!

Fireflies are the most abundant luminous insects in the tropics and are a source of great research interest. However, the complex preparation of the insects for shipment makes it unlikely that they will be overcollected in the near future. If the luminous lizards described by Ivan T. Sanderson could be "rediscovered" perhaps they too could be investigated, but although many visits have been made to the Aripo caves in Trinidad, where Sanderson claimed he saw them, none has ever been seen.

A similar enigmatic failure to verify early claims is the case of the alligator bugs of South America. Because of their uncanny resemblance to an alligator, these plant-sucking insects are illustrated in almost all the books that deal with mimicry. But what is really strange is that when the insect was first described, it was named the great lantern fly and credited with being luminous. Peter Parley wrote in 1837, "This beautiful insect is a native of Surinam and many other parts of South America and during the night diffuses so strong a phosphoric splendor from its head or lantern that it may be employed for the purpose of a candle or torch; and it is said that three or four of these insects tied to the top of a stick, are frequently used by travellers for that purpose." How odd that no modern naturalist has ever reported having seen these insects give out light.

In Trinidad, the elaterid fireflies of the genus *Pyrophorus* give out a great deal of light from a pair of spots on the thorax and a third at the tip of the abdomen. One of my sons was returning to boarding school at a time when the insects were common. What a riot it would cause to take some back to school! With my foolish acquiescence, a cake-tin full of fireflies was smuggled on board the night-flight to London. Alas, youthful enthusiasm triumphed over caution and he took a peep inside to see how the insects were enjoying their flight. By day they had been inactive and tractable, but by night they were rejuvenated and immediately filled the passenger compartment with winking beads of light. The stewardess's flight manual was silent on the subject of how to deal with firefly hysteria over the Atlantic!

To the stranger, the tropical rain forest at night is an awesome place, for there is so much mysterious activity. Not knowing at whom the activity is directed, it is easy to believe that it is directed toward oneself. In fact, the animals are all too busy going about their own private business to pay attention to us, for we are a trivial part of their world even if they are a significant part of ours.

Above. *This katydid (Copiphorinae) is nocturnal and hides by day on foliage, so the vivid colors seen during this gymnastic display performed in Sabah are normally concealed. Presumably, this performance advertises unpalatability, or reminds the predator which disturbs it during the day of prior distasteful experiences with similar-looking insects.*

Below. *Since the eighteenth century, naturalists have debated the function of the curious features of planthoppers (Fulgoridae) such as this* Laternaria phosphorea *from Peru. Variously called alligator, crocodile, or peanut bugs on account of the appearance of the head, it is hardly credible that predators have such human perceptions. Yet, the likeness is remarkable. The real eyes are inconspicuous and at the posterior margin of the "head." The head of the crocodile contains only air and fatty tissue, so unless the appearance is truly significant, we can ascribe no function to it at all. During the night, alligator bugs suck the juices of plants with their hypodermic mouth parts, although we do not know the identity of the plant species on which they feed.*

Cheating the Reaper

The shortage of food in the rain forest, whether on the forest floor or in the canopy, makes life a constant struggle. Plant toxins have forced herbivores either to be selective in their choice of foods or to develop immunity to their effects. Some insects are not only unaffected by plant poisons but have even acquired the ability to store them in order to protect themselves from their predators. Even so, few animals die of old age—the competition to stay alive is too keen. Ecologists have distinguished between two basic types of competition: rivalry for natural resources such as food, nesting sites, or territories (termed K-selection); and strategies for avoiding falling as prey (termed r-selection). An example of each type of selection will make the distinction clear, although rarely is an animal species exposed to only one type of selection. Usually, the hazards of living are a balance between the two.

The gorilla is a good example of a K-selected animal. It is a rain-forest herbivore which, because of its size, has few enemies. Even the juveniles are rendered safe from the attacks of predators by the protection of adults. However, the gorillas' great bulk demands that they spend a large proportion of their time and effort in feeding on a large selection of foliage, fruit, and seeds. Only by eating very young shoots and a few mature leaves of many species do they avoid the ill-effects of plant toxins. Gorillas can afford to have low birth rates and long lives only because their losses to predation are small. Their limiting factor is the supply of natural resources.

In contrast, most butterflies are preyed upon by a large number of enemies and are a good example of r-selected organisms. The eggs are parasitized by tiny wasps and eaten by both chewing and sucking insects; the caterpillars are eaten by birds and lizards and parasitized by wasps and flies; the chrysalids are eaten by any insectivore that finds them; and the adult butterflies are taken by spiders, lizards, and birds. Butterflies are rarely limited by lack of food, either as caterpillars or adults—their problem is living long enough to enjoy it! Such a challenge to survival is met by the female laying a large number of eggs to compensate for the massive losses along the road to maturity. Such populations which are limited by predation are r-selected.

The strategies to reduce attrition that have been developed by r-selected animals provide a fascinating spectrum of relationships. Among the most obvious techniques is that of protective coloration. We can distinguish several objectives in animal coloration that can broadly be grouped into passive and active. Passive coloration is designed to avoid being recognized as a food item, either by blending in with the background and becoming invisible, or by masquerading as a visible nonfood item. Active coloration leads the predator to believe that the animal, although clearly visible and identifiable, is hazardous and best avoided.

Passive coloration includes disruptive patterns that break up the outline or solid appearance of animals and makes them difficult to identify against their natural background. For example, many species of birds, lizards, and snakes have a bar of dark pigment horizontally in front of and behind the eye. This stripe renders the eye less conspicuous, for the eye is the one body structure that cannot be camouflaged or covered without impairing efficiency. Just as military aircraft, vessels, and vehicles are painted with stripes or blotches to break up their form, so also we find forest animals similarly camouflaged. The color patterns seem unexpectedly gaudy and brilliant in the hand or laboratory, but on sun-flecked foliage or the forest floor their owners become all but invisible.

Counter-shading is common in both aquatic and terrestrial animals, for the lighter belly negates the shadow cast by the upper body and renders the mass flat and lacking in solidity when viewed from the side. From above, the dark back blends with the ground, while from below the belly shines like the sky. However, small animals that rest on twigs or leaf stalks are usually not counter-shaded, for they are likely to be seen against a background of foliage from whatever angle they are viewed.

An alternate passive strategy to being camouflaged is to assume the appearance of an object that is not a part of the enemy's normal diet. Birds continually bypass caterpillars masquerading as broken twigs or fecal smears, katydids as leaves or lichens, membracids as thorns, and mantids as flowers. Again, these techniques are effective only as long as the animal behaves appropriately. A leaflike katydid resting by day on a flower head would leave very few offspring to which its bad habits could be passed.

In the few insects that have been investigated, laboratory experiments suggest that the brain is programmed to keep the insect active on any but an appropriate background. A flying insect does not select a suitable landing site by exercising choice; it is just unable to rest until a suitable background has appeared in its field of view. It has been noticed that when birds find an unexpected food source, such as a twiglike caterpillar, they will energetically inspect all the twigs on the tree. Hence, it is an advantage for such mimetic insects to be widely dispersed, for if the rewards for such diligent searching were really profitable, the birds might adopt this feeding technique as a habit and the mimetic advantage would be lost.

Active coloration enhances the protection afforded by being poisonous or equipped with venom and only realizes its full potential when prospective predators learn to recognize the organisms on sight. Ideally, a single experience with a protected animal should be sufficient to deter later attacks on any other member of that species. Thus, only one individual should be sacrificed in the education of the predator. Evolutionists believe that the reason that protected animals such as bees, wasps, and smelly insects are so brightly and distinctively colored is to facilitate this learning process. The most common colors of such "warningly" patterned animals are various combinations of red, black, and yellow. The frequency with which venomous or poisonous animals exhibit red, black,

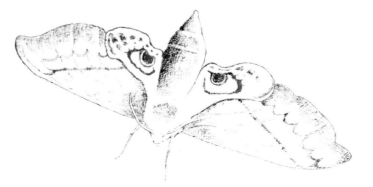

Preceding pages. (left) *Even when one has time to examine this resting moth* (Tarsolepis sommeri: *Notodontidae*) *from Mount Kinabalu really closely, the effective shading and scale tufts defy the mind to grasp its true shape.*

(right) *Who would think that this object, dangling at the end of a dead liana and twirling in the wind, is an edible moth? Notice how the wings are held away and downward from the body and the abdomen is elevated—a most unmothlike stance. This unidentified member of the Mimallonidae is from Belém, Brazil.*

and yellow patterns has led investigators to wonder if the recognition of these warning colors is instinctive.

Susan Smith, working at the Organization for Tropical Studies site in Costa Rica, has recently published the results of an interesting experiment involving hand-reared turquoise-browed motmot birds. In random sequence, the birds were presented with colored snakelike models, each painted with one of three contrasting patterns: red, black, and yellow longitudinal stripes; red, black, and yellow rings; or blue and green rings. The birds pecked frequently and without hesitation at the blue-and-green model and at the one striped with red, black, and yellow. Attacks on the red-, black-, and yellow-ringed model numbered less than 5 percent of the attacks on any of the other two. Remember that these birds had never been in the wild. Did the naive birds avoid the red-, black-, and yellow-ringed model by instinct? Is it coincidence that the same pattern of colored rings is characteristic of the venomous coral snake? More experiments are needed to answer these questions with confidence. Superficially, the explanation of the red, black, and yellow patterns of venomous animals as those of warning coloration seems satisfactory. But when individual situations are examined critically, the explanations become deficient.

Coral snakes occur throughout the American tropics and subtropics as predators on the forest floor. When they bite, or more accurately chew, the very potent nerve-paralyzing venom is injected through a pair of rather short teeth fixed at the front of the upper jaw. They are all, without exception, colored with various combinations of red, black, and yellow rings that completely encircle the body and tail. From our biased human standpoint, such a pattern is truly conspicuous, but coral snakes are all nocturnal. By day, snake collectors find them only by turning over rocks, logs, tree stumps, and forest litter. At whom, then, are these colors directed? Do their natural enemies seek them by day or by night? What, in fact, are their natural enemies? Do their enemies have color vision? If so, can they detect colors in the weak intensities of twilight or by the light of the moon? Humans are thought to have good color vision, yet we are unable to see their colors after dusk. We know almost nothing about the biology of coral snakes. The few observations recorded indicate that they are at least occasionally caught by storks and birds of prey and that they themselves feed on other snakes, even including members of their own species. There is so much that we do not know!

Because the nocturnal habits of coral snakes seem to undercut the argument that the bright colors act only as a warning, other explanations have been offered. One biologist has explained away the colors by claiming that the pigments are purely inert waste products that have been dumped in the skin and are without significance. The banding is alleged to have value as a source of confusion to a predator watching it pass through the forest litter. I can confirm that they are hard to catch at night, and that the banding does contribute to the difficulty of judging exactly where they are.

The coral-snake plot thickens! From the arid climates of the southwestern United States through the tropical rain forests of Amazonia to Argentina, coral snakes are found in the company of other similarly banded snakes that either have no venom at all or have it conducted only through teeth at the back of the mouth. The back-fanged snakes have copious quantities of highly toxic venom, but because of the posterior position of the teeth near the hinge line of the jaws it seems unlikely that animals larger than their normal prey would be affected. The venom of back-fanged snakes can be effective, as was shown by the death of the famous herpetologist Carl P. Schmidt following a bite from a South African boomslang *(Dispholidus typus)* which he handled carelessly.

Traditional evolutionary theory offers a pair of contrasting explanations for the similar appearance of different species of animals. The first explanation, named after the English naturalist H. W. Bates who first proposed it in 1862, maintains that one organism (the model) is protected from predators by being venomous or toxic and adopts a characteristic color pattern that predators can recognize immediately. The other organism (the mimic) is not protected at all, but by acquiring a color pattern that mimics that of the model, it gains a measure of protection by being mistaken for the model by educated predators. Of course, an inexperienced predator will attempt to eat whichever organism it encounters, and will continue to do so until it attacks a protected model. Thereafter, having become educated, it should avoid both model and mimic.

If the model is only mildly distasteful or venomous, the presence of numerous innocuous mimics will serve to dilute the effectiveness of the model's protection. The predator may consider the high probability of a palatable meal well worth the risk of only a moderate amount of discomfort, particularly if alternative food items are uncommon. However, if the model is violently toxic or venomous, even with relatively high proportions of mimics in the population the predators may feel that the risk is simply not worth taking and the mimics are protected.

The second explanation of mimicry follows the reasoning of H. W. Müller, who in 1878 felt that the Batesian concept was inadequate to cover all situations. Müller supposed that the smaller the number of different warning patterns that the predators have to remember, the faster they will learn them. Moreover, the possession of a common pattern by two or more species of protected animals would enable the predators to become more thoroughly educated by experience to avoid any of the species in the mimetic complex.

Applying these concepts to the coral-snake situation, we have three kinds of snake: nonvenomous species such as the king snake (*Lampropeltis*), the potentially venomous back-fanged false coral (*Erythrolamprus*), and the fully venomous coral snake (*Micrurus*). Bates could have argued

Left. *The color patterns of coral snakes have puzzled biologists for over a century. Why are the snakes so conspicuously adorned? Is it warning coloration? Is it a source of concealment on the sun-flecked forest floor? These are difficult questions to answer, for their nocturnal display is seen by few, if any, animals with good color vision. Periodically the debate explodes into a fury of controversy. The patterns of coral snakes vary, but are almost always a combination of red, yellow, and black annuli, as seen in this* Micrurus nigrofasciatus.

Above. *When moving over the forest floor, these lepidoptera larvae in Java maintain constant contact with each other, sliding over one another as they walk. The overall effect is that of a shiny, slithering snake. Mimicry? Perhaps.*

that both the king snake and the false coral were Batesian mimics of the venomous coral and neither was capable of deterring a predator on its own, but each was afforded protection by being mistaken for the coral by experienced predators. Müller, on the other hand, could have maintained that only the harmless king snake was a Batesian mimic, for the false coral and the true coral were both protected Müllerian models and resembled each other in order to reduce the number of warning patterns the predators had to learn.

The critical question concerns the lethality of the back-fanged snakes. Against its enemies, is it protected or not? The German herpetologist Robert Mertens has offered a third possible explanation. He suggests that the back-fanged snake is the only type of snake in the complex that can educate, the king snake having no venom and the true coral being lethal and thus killing the predator before it can learn. Thus the false coral is the model and both the king snake and the true coral are mimics. This situation has become known as Mertensian mimicry after its proponent.

A piece of information that needs to be considered is that on the island of Tobago, some twenty-one miles (34 km) northeast of Trinidad, the back-fanged false coral lives in the absence of either the innocuous king snake or the true coral. We do not know, of course, for how long examples of the other two snakes have been absent. The interesting fact is that the Tobagonian false coral is ringed only on the tail, the trunk pattern consisting of yellow spots surrounded by black borders on a red background. Does this suggest that in the absence of the true coral to serve as a model, the false coral can extract no advantage from being warningly colored? To answer such questions we have to know much more about the biology of all the snakes involved, but the secretive nocturnal habits and small population sizes of coral snakes make them difficult to study.

Butterflies, on the contrary, are abundant, diurnal, easy to rear in captivity, and all exhibit similar mimetic problems. It is well over a century since Bates journeyed up the Amazon and observed that more than ninety butterfly species not only appeared similar one to another, to the extent that some could barely be distinguished, but they belonged to more than a dozen different families. It was based on his study of these butterflies that Bates proposed the mimetic relationships outlined in the discussion of mimicry in coral snakes. The butterflies examined by Bates were also patterned with red, black, and yellow. In the 1960s, Lincoln Brower of Amherst College designed a most ingenious experiment in an effort to determine whether these colors alone afforded protection from wild predators.

Through advertisements in butterfly- and moth-collector's journals, Brower purchased a large number of cocoons of the North American day-flying saturniid moth *Hyalophora promethea,* which is popular with amateur collectors for the attraction of the males by female scent. In their native haunts, the newly emerged females emit an odor that attracts males from distances of up to sixteen miles (26 km). The chemical secretion, properly termed a sex pheromone, is detected by receptors on the antennae of the male moths at dilutions of only a few parts of the active chemical per billion parts of air.

The cocoons were shipped in ice chests to Trinidad, where the refrigeration was continued until the adult moths were needed. By warming the cocoons and their enclosed pupae according to a carefully calculated schedule, the emergence of the adults was controlled so that about two hundred moths emerged each day over a period of three weeks. The Agricultural Department of the Trinidad and Tobago government was not disturbed by the importation of the insects because only the males were to be released.

As the insects emerged, single females were placed in individual wire-gauze cages with lobster-pot entrances. Cages containing the captive females were then hung from trees around the sides and entrance to the Arima Valley. Each day, males were released from a central point and allowed to fly away. Sooner or later, each of them encountered the odor of a captive virgin female, zeroed in on her cage, and became trapped. They could not actually reach the female because she was inside an inner gauze compartment. Most frustrating!

The heart of the experiment was that the released males were used only as vehicles for different color patterns. During the evening prior to being released, the males were painted with quick-drying enamel. Half of this group were painted bright red, black, and yellow and the other half with a similar weight of dull brown paint. It was hoped that by counting the number of each color type recovered at the cages, the effectiveness of the warning color pattern could be compared with that of a neutral color. About 25 percent of the 1,246 males released were recaptured, a very satisfactory figure for such an unusual experiment.

Although the insectivorous birds of the Arima Valley had seen red, black, and yellow butterflies, they had never seen these particular insects. Their novelty must have been obvious, for there the moths fly only between 3:30 and 4:00 in the afternoon and unlike any similar local insects they fly erratically and fast over the forest canopy. On the first day following release, the number of red–black–yellow moths recovered at the cages was more numerous than of their brown companions, presumably because more of the brown ones had been eaten by birds. However, by the morning following the third day of release, the numbers of the two patterns recovered were about equally divided and on every day thereafter the recapture rate of the red–black–yellow moths declined.

An interpretation of these data is that initially the birds looked warily at the red–black–yellow moths because previous experience had taught them that such colors were associated with distastefulness. However, they attacked and ate some of those painted brown and found them palatable. Encouraged by the similar flight pattern, they then ate a red–black–yellow moth and found that equally delicious. As

Following pages. (top left) *It is not what you do, but the way that you do it! This little moth extends its front legs, wraps its hind legs with its wings, and tucks up its middle legs under its body. With a recurved abdomen the effect is extraordinary. This cryptic pose is being displayed by a plume moth (Pterophoridae) in Costa Rica.*

(bottom left) *Even on only marginally suitable backgrounds, the tufts of elongate scales and counter-shading of the moth* Crinodes bellatrix *(Notodontidae) from Amazonas will probably enable it to escape detection during the day.*

(right) *If disturbed by day, this* Automeris moloneyi *(Saturniidae) from Manaus, Brazil, has a second line of defense. The overly inquisitive bird probes the "dead leaf" and is greeted with the flash of a large pair of eyespots. During its surprise, the moth flies off, resettles, and perhaps escapes.*

Opposite. Parides *(Papilionidae) is known to be highly distasteful to birds. The specimen shown here, from Trinidad, is feeding on freshly opened flowers of* Lantana camera *(Verbenaceae), a popular flower with butterflies. Notice that the butterfly is feeding on a flower at the edge of the flower head.* Lantana *secretes only nectar in the most recently opened flowers at the edge of the head; the inner flowers are nectarless but remain in bloom to increase the floral display.*

Following pages. Helicopis acis *(Riodinidae) from Amazonas is cunningly protected, for the hind wings are drawn out into a pair of fake antennae, complete with white tip as a valueless target for insectivorous birds. One might construe the hind-wing markings as spiderlike, but that may be taking mimetic speculation too far.*

the multicolored individuals were more conspicuous, they suffered greater and greater losses as more and more birds came to regard them as potential prey. And it was not long before the birds were sitting over the entrances to the cages, picking off the males without regard to color as they homed in on the females. When Brower set up the same experiment at the same site a year later, birds could be found sitting on the cages before a single moth had been released. To be called a "bird-brain" may not be so derogatory after all!

In all these situations, the predator has to survive in order to become educated. Death is a poor learning experience. Or is it possible that one predator can witness the demise of another and learn without actually experiencing the punishment himself? The answer to this question is pertinent to any discussion involving mimicry with such potentially lethal animals as coral snakes. There is little relevant experimental evidence, but such visual learning does at least seem possible.

The animal behaviorist Peter H. Klopfer kept domesticated ducks in two concentric wire enclosures so that the birds in the outer pen could see the activities of those in the inner one. In the inner cage, some of the water troughs were electrified so they administered a painful, but not fatal, electric shock to any bird that lowered its beak into the water. The birds soon learned to avoid those particular troughs and drank only from the others. After a few weeks, the birds that had been in the outer cage were placed in the inner one and vice versa. The newly arrived inner-cage birds avoided the electrified troughs without testing them! They had been watching through the wire and had learned by observing the fate of their fellows.

Unraveling the mysteries of mimicry is one of the most intriguing and stimulating aspects of tropical biology. There are facets of interest for geneticists, ecologists, evolutionists, and biochemists, as well as for the natural historian. The most involved and complex mimetic relationships are to be found in the tropical rain forests, for it is there that the diversity of animal and plant species is the greatest in the world.

Opposite. (top) *The crowned katydids (Tettigoniidae) are the largest ones in the world, some species reaching over four inches (10 cm) long.* Steirodon ponderosum *illustrated here is from Manaus.*

(bottom) *Perhaps one of the most effectively camouflaged insects is the katydid* Acanthodes, *seen here in Venezuela.*

Above. *The function of jet-black spots on the backs of some tropical katydids have long puzzled entomologists. The juxtaposition of this katydid nymph from West Africa with holes in a leaf suggests a novel form of mimicry. Is this insect mimicking holes in a leaf?*

Opposite. (top) *Not even the most extreme evolutionist would argue that this* New Guinea moth (Apsarasa nigrocaerulia) *is mimicking the imprint of a hiking boot!*

(bottom) *On the jungle floor in Belém, Brazil,* Automeris io (Saturniidae) *is not invisible but not readily recognizable for what it really is—a moth. If it remains motionless by day it may survive to live a little at night!*

Above. (left) *Tortoise beetles,* Batonota spinosa, *from Bolivia are inconspicuous on the spiny bark of a silk-cotton tree.*

(right) *Hungry birds would easily overlook* Chloropteryx albidata, *provided it always chose a lichen-encrusted trunk for its daytime resting place.*

Following pages. *This walking-stick insect (Phasmatodea) from New Guinea depends on threadlike dimensions to escape the attention of its enemies. What the minute red-eyed fly is doing on its most posterior tip is a mystery.*

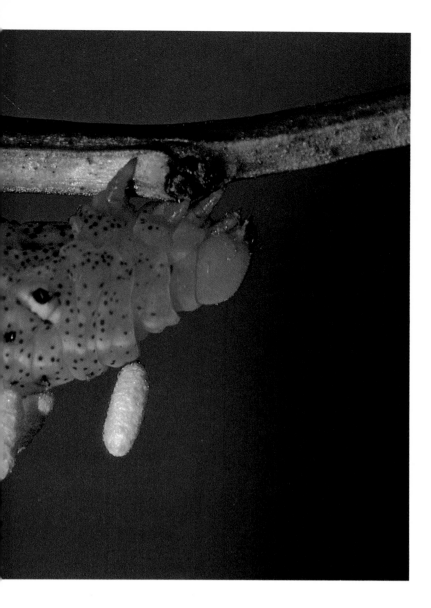

Left. *No color pattern will protect caterpillars from the attention of parasitic wasps, which search vigorously for their victims. The wasps lay one or more eggs inside the caterpillar, each egg sometimes hatching into thirty or more larvae, which consume all but the most important parts of the caterpillar. When the wasp larvae are fully developed, they eat their way out of the caterpillar's skin and spin silken cocoons on the outside. After a few days they emerge as adult wasps. The caterpillar always dies. The example here shows a hawkmoth caterpillar (Sphingidae) parasitized with the cocoons of* Trichogramma *(Hymenoptera) in Venezuela.*

Below. (left & right) *The larvae of the chrysomelid beetle* Hilarocassis *from Manaus, Brazil, live gregariously and camouflage themselves with their own feces!*

Following pages. *The soft, downy appearance belies the severely urticating properties of the hairs of these Megalopygidae larvae from the Amazon basin. The human hand that crushes these caterpillars will swell up within minutes and remain bloated for several hours. The pain is excruciating.*

Above. *Green is a safe color to be in the rain forest, particularly if the surface texture resembles the venation of a leaf. Not much is known about tropical planthoppers such as this fulgorid from Manaus, Brazil.*

Above. (right) *Scale insects are notoriously difficult to identify, but the brown scablike animals at the tip of this leaf in Sabah, on Mount Kinabalu, are mussel scales. The diminutive white insects, each covered in wax, presumably have recently emerged from eggs under the mussel-scale armor. It is not known why all the white insects are facing the same way.*

Right. *Almost every beginning entomology student is confronted with a sawfly larva (Hymenoptera) during the end-of-term examination, for the larvae are easily confused with the caterpillars of butterflies and moths. These are feeding on the epidermis of a leaf in Ghana. The green leaf tissue can be seen in their alimentary canal through their semitransparent body wall. Their feces still contain a great deal of chlorophyll which has not been digested. Presumably, their group feeding behavior affords some measure of protection from their enemies, although how it is effected is not obvious.*

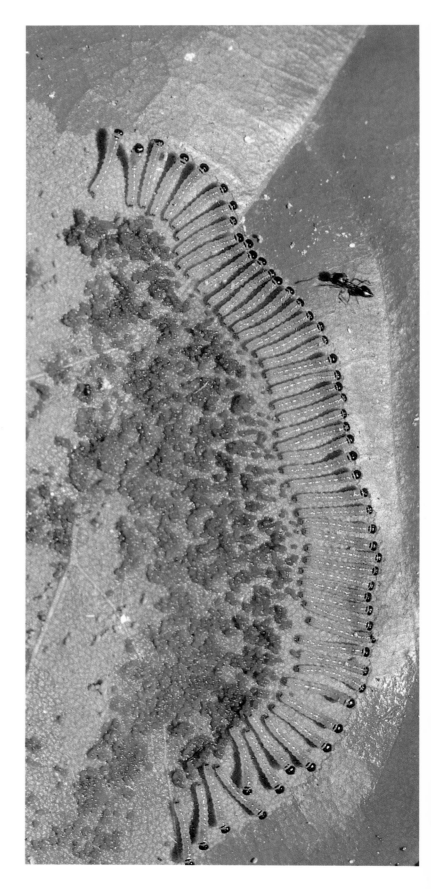

Above. *Although conspicuous, these waxen threads are not relished by birds and other predators. Both the mature stages and nymphs of whiteflies (Aleyrodidae) are protected by a covering of wax. This early-stage nymph of* Aleyrodes *is feeding on an orchid leaf in Colombia. Whiteflies are well known to horticulturists as serious, hard-to-control pests, partly because the waxy covering wards off aqueous insecticides.*

Following pages. *At first sight, these small flies in Ghana seem trapped in the spider's web, however the flies are free to leave — and do very readily if they are disturbed — only to return to the web a few minutes later. The relationship between these* Forcipomyia *flies, which are pollinators of cacao, and these spiders is a mystery.*

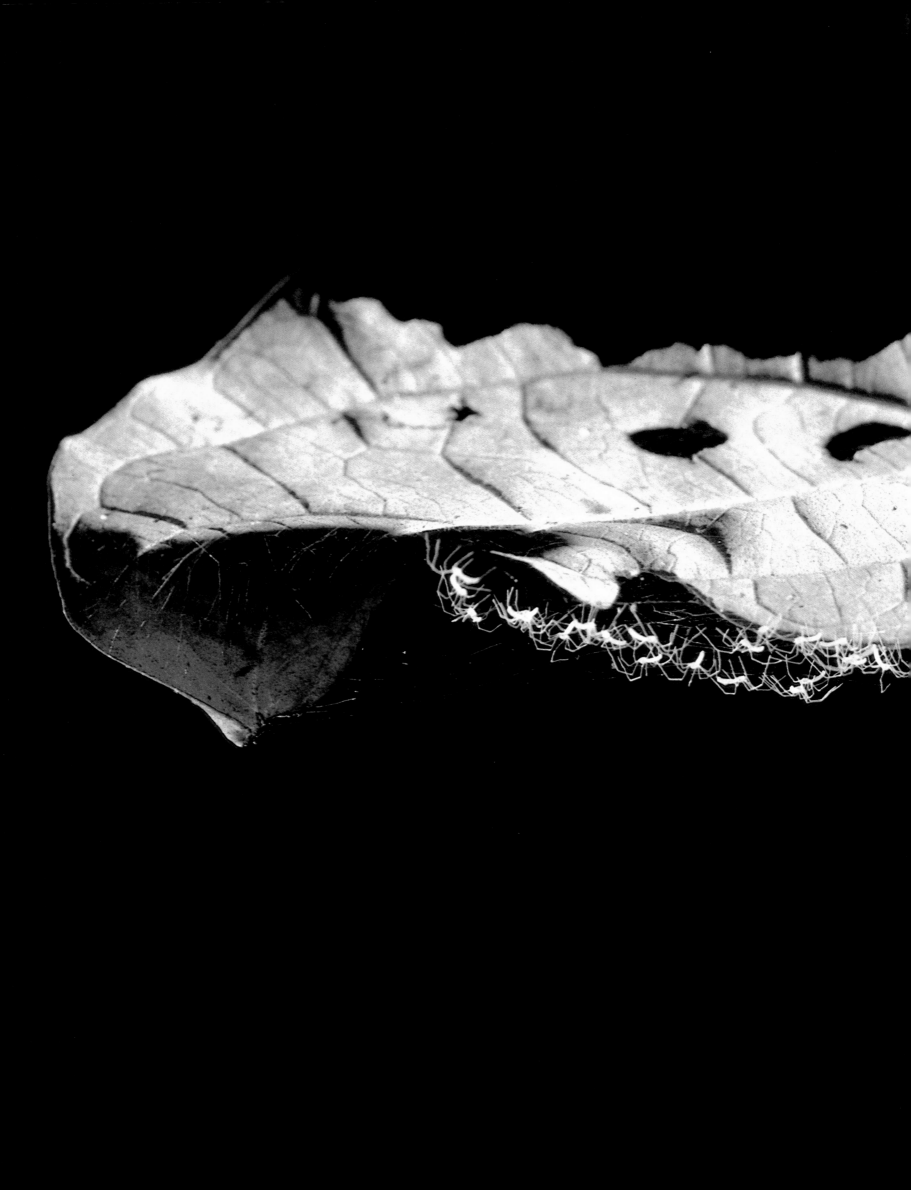

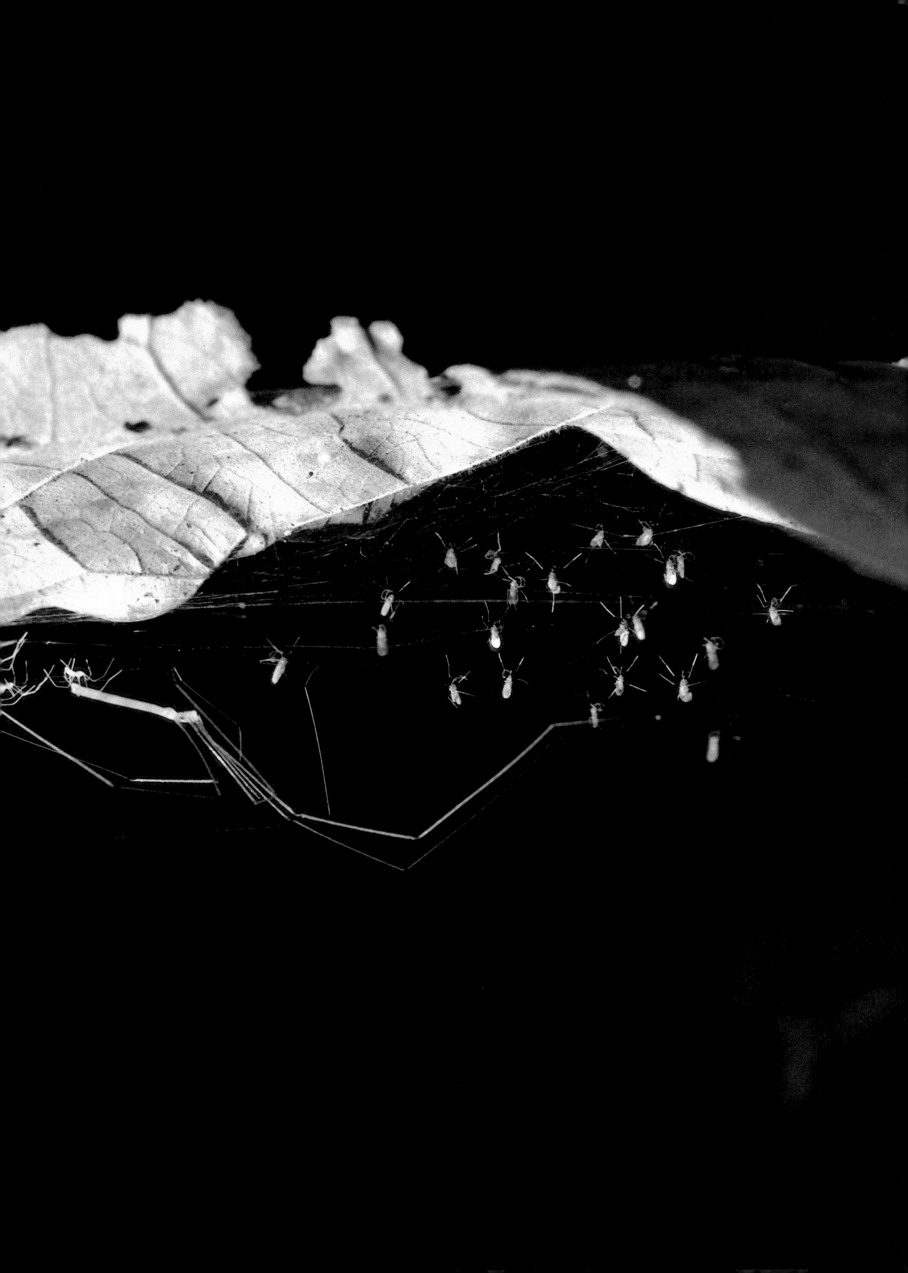

Right. *Spiders, particularly in the tropics, have been seriously neglected by scientists's studies. This species of* Cyclosa *from West Africa has unusual thickening in the center of its orb web. Three meals are packaged up for later consumption.*

Bottom. *To anyone such as myself who abhors spiders, the thought of a twenty-foot web (6 m) is horrifying; however, the webs built by the communal* Cyrtophora moluccensis *spiders of New Guinea frequently reach that size. The thought of walking into one gives me instant gooseflesh!*

Top right. *Termite workers have a very thin cuticle which is unable to protect their delicate body tissues from damage by ultraviolet light, so they forage in the open only at night and by day they live inside their nests or in their food material, which is connected to their nest by an earthen tunnel. The tunnel illustrated in Manaus, Brazil, has had the roof collapsed to show the workers traveling from a log to their nest.*

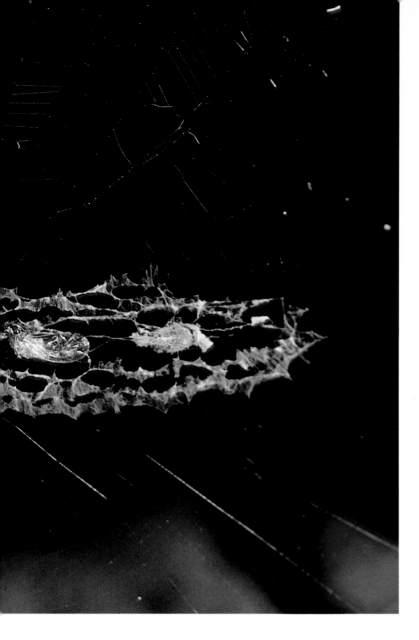

Above. *In order to find the royal chamber of a termite nest, the interested student must dig for hours. Here is the queen in all her glory. When she founded the colony, she was of similar size to that of her consort, who is still at her side. The original abdominal plates can be seen on the queen's back, now appearing as islands in a sea of expanded membrane, for her obesity is due to the extraordinary growth of her ovaries, which can lay up to two thousand eggs each day. This is the royal couple and one worker of* Macrotermes bellicosus *in Ghana. Some queens have been known to live up to fifty years. Notice the red color of the soil, typical of tropical lateritic earth.*

Left. *The outside of this nest of* Protopolybia pumila *from Panama is being examined by its inhabitants for damage after a rainstorm. If the nest leaks, the wasps drink the floodwater and regurgitate it at the entrance to the nest.*

Above. *The relationship between the scarab beetle (*Golofa porteri*) and the fly is not known. The fly could be feeding on the exudate from the damaged bamboo, but that does not explain why it is resting on the back of the beetle. The male beetles compete for females and will drop down bamboo stems, in the manner of children sliding down banisters, to dislodge an adversary lower down.*

(right) *Large red mites, such as this specimen found at an altitude of five thousand feet (1,525 m) in New Guinea, are common throughout the humid and arid tropical habitats, but they have received little study and almost nothing is known about them.*

Rain-forest Vandal

If the evolutionists are to be believed, our human ancestors were hunting and gathering on the plains of Africa three and a half million years ago. The acid soil of tropical forests inhibits fossilization, so although we do not know much about human occupation there we are able to follow a thread of human survival through to the present day. Our contemporary rain-forest dwellers carry out foraging practices that may have remained unchanged for thousands of years. Their numbers are small and their civilizations modest by comparison with the remainder of the world. Why do the pygmies of the Congo and the native tribes of upper Amazonia have such a poor history of farming? The answer is not hard to find, for the fertility of rain-forest soils is a frustrating deception.

For centuries, temperate-zone explorers and adventurers have brought back vivid descriptions of the richness of the rain forests of the Amazon, the Congo, and Southeast Asia. Modern tropical politicians and engineers are still committed to the mythical notion that the rain-forest soils are a fertile source of wealth awaiting human development. At this point in the earth's history, the rain forest is the last remaining resource that has not come under human domination. The rest of the world, from the oil below the arctic tundra to the manganese nodules on the ocean floor, is being vigorously exploited. The obvious clue to the poor agricultural potential of the rain forest is that no sophisticated civilization has been able to exist for long in a rain-forest environment. Seed agriculture, based on wheat, barley, and rye, began about eleven thousand years ago at the eastern end of the Mediterranean. Prior to that time there is only fragmentary evidence that some tropical root crops, such as yams, sweet potatoes, and taro, were cultivated in Southeast Asia. Since then, apart from some fruits, only the South American cassava has been added to our tropical menu. Rice, maize, guinea corn, squash, and potatoes are all subtropical or temperate in origin. The history of tropical crops is fully described by John Purseglove in a superb series of books which he began when he was professor of botany at the Imperial College of Tropical Agriculture in Trinidad.

The rain-forest ecosystem is extremely fragile. The nutritional input is minimal, being confined to a modest amount falling in rain- and wind-blown detritus with a small quantity of it washing in from neighboring areas in surface runoff. The rain forest feeds on itself, the same nutrients being recycled over and over again. Take away the forest and you take away the soil fertility with it, for more than 90 percent of the nutrients in a tropical rain forest are in the standing crop of vegetation.

Rapid recycling is not confined to the movement of nutrients. The water that falls through the forest canopy is taken up immediately by the roots of epiphytes and ground plants. Then, by transpiration, the water evaporates from the leaves and into the atmosphere. As this atmospheric water vapor rises away from the heat of the canopy, it cools, condenses, and falls again as rain. The same water is recycled, over and over again, sometimes as many as twenty times. At each falling, some water is absorbed by the soil and finds its way to the sea, but its residence time is extended enormously by the cyclical delays. If the forests were to be removed, the water carried in by the moist sea breezes would fall only once and the area would become much more dry. Therefore, the effects of clear-cutting the rain forests over a wide area would be dramatic and would lead to four predictable serious problems.

First, the exposure of the ground to direct sunlight would raise the temperature of the soil from its normal 68°F (20°C) to over 115°F (46°C). The soil chemistry would be accelerated and the processes of degradation would proceed apace. Lateritic soils would become as hard as brick and quite unsuitable for any agricultural purpose other than roadmaking. Second, the direct impact of the rain on the unprotected soil surface would lead to acute erosion by the rapid runoff of the water. The creeks, streams, and rivers would be subjected to unprecedented burdens of silt, which would scour out their vegetation and decimate the population of freshwater animals. The course of rivers would be altered and many waterways rendered unnavigable. Life in the deltas would suffer from the deposition of silt over biologically active mud flats. Third, the soil fungi, bacteria, and other decomposer organisms would be unable to withstand the changes in their environment. Instead of a cool, moist, dark habitat they would be exposed to the intense insolation of the tropical sun with its attendant high temperatures, desiccation, and ultraviolet light. Few decomposers from the original forest could withstand such a traumatic change, and breakdown of litter would be slowed dramatically. Last, the soil would be infertile. Whatever nutrients were in the soil at the time of clear-cutting would be washed out by rainfall or blown away by high winds, which would reach ground level without hindrance for the first time in the history of the forest.

In the undisturbed tropical rain forest, peasant agriculture has been reasonably successful only because the acreage under cultivation at any one time has been small. Typically, the so-called slash-and-burn style of shifting cultivation consists of felling the C- and B-level trees just above the top of their buttresses and clearing all the understory vegetation over an area of about one quarter of an acre. The brush is then burned and the ashes scattered over the land. While the plot is small, the protection afforded by the surrounding forest prevents the ashes from being blown or washed away. A crop of yams (*Dioscorea*), taro (*Colocasia*), cassava (*Manihot*), cowpea (*Vigna*), sorghum (*Sorghum*), or millet (*Panicum*) is planted and left until harvest. A small plot within the rain forest is almost totally devoid of weeds and although secondary forest growth will appear, the crop will grow away from its competitors and produce a harvest. The same plot will be used for successive croppings for perhaps as long as four years, although after two years the yields will begin to decline. Usually a new plot is cut after three years and the original plot is

Preceding pages. *Grassland fires are a natural phenomenon, but fires are frequently set by agriculturists in order to kill off surface vegetation prior to planting or to promote the sprouting of soft shoots for cattle pasture. The increased number of fires exerts a continuous pressure on the edges of the forest, for the trees are killed and replaced by grasses. The forests most severely affected are the riparian forests that border water courses, for they have great length but little width and are vulnerable to damage by fire.*

Following pages. (left) *The Indian elephant (*Elephas maximus*) is almost extinct in the wild but is still abundant in domestication, where it is used for a variety of heavy work. However, with the advent of mechanized tractors, the need for elephants will decline and the old traditions will be lost. Mahouts, like the old man illustrated, represent an endangered vocation.*

(top right) *This capybara is lucky; she is in a zoo. In Colombia, the capybara is being systematically hunted to extinction. The carcasses are processed for human or canine food at such a rate that the world's largest rodent soon will be yet another animal whose existence is dependent entirely on zoos.*

(bottom right) *The lowland gorilla of western and central tropical African rain forests is threatened with extinction. Not only is it hunted but, more seriously, its habitat is being destroyed. The territories of forest animals must be certain minimum sizes for effective maintenance of a viable population, and in most cases the existing park reserves are insufficiently large. This silver-back male is over ten years old and enjoying life in a zoo. The usual situation in which an obese and neurotic gorilla passes its days in a tiled cell is one of the saddest sights. In the wild, gorillas are docile, gentle, intelligent, and loving—qualities that are rarely seen on public display.*

abandoned for ten years or more. This mode of agriculture can indefinitely support about ten persons per square kilometer. The trouble comes when population pressure demands that the land be put into cultivation more frequently than its rejuvenation processes can sustain, which is now a common situation in the tropics.

In order to meet the food needs of a burgeoning population the use of synthetic fertilizers has been explored but has been found to be uneconomical. The problem is partly their high cost when delivered to remote tropical sites, and partly that the structure of tropical soils does not hold nutrients well. The heavy rainfall leeches out the fertilizer within a very short period of time, and at present our domesticated food crops do not have the mycorrhizal associations that seem beneficial for rapid nutrient uptake by forest plants. A possible solution to the problem is to encourage mixed farming, for the tropical Southeast Asian pig (*Sus vittatus*) is an amenable forest animal and would provide a supply of meat and natural fertilizer for little investment.

As a means of both increasing food production and providing work for the poverty-stricken inhabitants of northeastern Brazil, the government has embarked on a scheme to develop settlement farming in the Amazonian rain forests. The plan is to build a network of roads and subsidize agricultural small-holdings, which will ultimately cover the whole region. Much of the plan has already been implemented, but some weakening of commitment has appeared as the yields of the earlier settlements have begun to decline. Ecologists Robert Goodland of the World Bank and Howard Irvin of the New York Botanical Garden blasted off a warning of the catastrophe-to-come in their timely book *Amazon Jungle: Green Hell to Red Desert,* and Harald Sioli of the Max-Planck Institute, who has spent much of his professional life in Amazonia, appealed to reason in the Association for Tropical Biology's landmark review of African and South American tropical-forest ecosystems.

Forestry is an alternative to agriculture for the human use of the tropical rain forests, although extreme caution must again be exercised, for any kind of clear-cutting practices would result in the disaster just outlined. The optimum gain would come from the selective cutting of favored timbers, backed up with a planned system of replanting. The forest as a whole must be disturbed as little as possible. We would have to be patient, for it will take nothing less than eighty years for a mature tree to be replaced by one of harvestable size. The spacing of the trees must not be disturbed or the incidence of disease and insect attack may rise. Diversity must not be reduced or there may be a breakdown in pollinating mechanisms and the structure of the forests will change. The modern developer from the temperate zone is not prepared to wait. He sees the redwood forests of western California and visualizes pure stands of teak, mora, or mahogany. He forgets that the northern winter cuts back the populations of insects and pathogens every year. Such single-minded application of temperate forestry has been attempted in the past and has met with failure. Following the rubber boom at the turn of the century, Amazonian rubber plantations and their temperate-educated developers were wiped out by disease. Only by raising the rubber trees in Southeast Asia, where they are free from their natural enemies, is it possible to grow commercial crops successfully.

William Meijer has given us a graphic account of the devastation of the tropical rain forests in Southeast Asia. One half of all the rain forests, more than twenty million acres, are leased to lumber companies. Not content with recklessly cutting the preferred tree species, they are poisoning the "valueless" trees in the vain hope that they will be replaced by those that are of commercial use. Of course, the disturbed areas become filled with secondary growth species replete with vines, for the seedlings of the timber trees cannot survive after the opening of the canopy. When one remembers that many dipterocarp trees flower and release seeds only at irregular intervals of up to twenty years, it is not inconceivable that some species will become extinct. The ruthless quest for the dipterocarps that yield "Philippine mahogany" for the veneer plywood industry is destroying a whole ecosystem. Think of that when you are paneling your basement!

It is not only in Southeast Asia that the rain forests are being destroyed. The cloud forests of Costa Rica are being cut to produce charcoal fuel and pasture. The montane forests in Central America are being replaced with coffee plantations, and the Amazon rain forests seem destined to be fermented into alcohol, which will then fuel Brazilian automobiles. In Africa, the riparian forests are constantly being eroded by man-made savanna fires. All over the tropics, ever-enlarging circles of barren dry earth are growing out of villages and settlements as wood, the most important human fuel, is harvested to maintain the exponential growth of human populations.

The destruction of the forests is only one aspect of the problem, for we have developed but a small number of tropical crops for human use. There are vast numbers of species that have never been investigated, some of which may have excellent potential as sources of food, drugs, or commercial products. Are we going to destroy them before we have even had a chance to examine them? The answer seems to be, "Yes." Where are we going to obtain new material for improving the strains of existing tropical fruits such as bananas, citrus, cacao, and beans if we eliminate their wild ancestors? We will lose the potential source of genes against disease, insect attack, and other desirable qualities.

Last, but in my mind by no means least, is the loss of wildlife. Almost all the larger animals are already endangered by a two-sided attack: they are hunted for meat or the commercial value of their hides and at the same time their habitats are being destroyed. Even if we wish to protect them, there will soon be nowhere for them to go. It seems likely that by the end of this century the only places on earth where rain-forest animals and plants will survive will be in zoos and botanical gardens.

How easy it is to sit in one's air-conditioned office and pontificate about the disasters about to befall our tropical wildlife. How different it would seem from the perspective of one of the billion people living in Southeast Asia. We forget how privileged we are. We can afford to become excited about traplining bats, mimetic butterflies, and social behavior in tapirs. To a hungry belly, a tapir means only one thing—food! An endangered Rajah Brooke's birdwing butterfly means money, and money means food. What hope is there? None, I fear. That is why we are so fortunate. We can join in the excitement of discovery for just another thirty years or so. After that, the story of the rain forest will be recorded only in picture books and slide shows. We can only hope that the words of François René de Chateaubriand (1768–1848) will be proven false: "Forests precede peoples and nations, deserts succeed them."

Above. *Rajah Brooke's birdwing* (Trogonoptera brookiana) *is protected by law in Borneo, but specimens still find their way into the collectors' shops in the United States and western Europe. Sometimes protection can so hike the commercial price that poachers take as many specimens as would have been taken in the absence of protection, and sometimes more.*

Right. *The clear-cutting of the forest can be seen in the middle of this picture taken near Wau, New Guinea, at six thousand feet (1,850 m). Clear-cutting is a viable practice in temperate climates with good soil fertility and moderate rainfall, but in the tropics it is an ecological disaster.*

Left. *In the Orient and Indonesia, lumbering is the dominant threat to the rain forest. The Dipterocarpaceae are so valued for the production of fine veneers sold under the name Philippine mahogany that the forests are being clear-cut just to extract a few valuable trees. Since the dipterocarps take eighty years to grow to maturity and fruit only at very long periods of time, their fate seems sealed.*

Above. *One of the growing industries in the tropics is the manufacture of charcoal. The fuel crisis is nowhere as acute as it is in the tropics, for the forests have been cut within a day's walk of almost every village on every continent. Charcoal is light, easily transportable, and provides heat for cooking. This charcoal site is in the middle of what used to be a Costa Rican cloud forest.*

Left. *Western children would be delighted to be allowed to live in this tree house in Sri Lanka. For the real-world occupants it is a full-time habitation; it is not a chosen residence but the only one available. With widespread poverty at this level, how can Westerners expect to protect wildlife resources for the future when they can be exploited by humans now?*

Nonbotanists can, perhaps, be forgiven for questioning how such a tree house would tolerate the continued growth of the tree. However, as lovers who have carved their initials in the bark of a sapling discover, although the passage of time may render the marks rather vague, they will be no higher from the ground than when they were fresh. The elongation of a trunk or branch takes place only at the tip of the shoots. The only growth which follows is increase in girth.

The tree is reminiscent of the African baobab, a widely distributed tree which stores water in its pulpy and ample trunk to tide it over periods of extended drought. During the dry season when all the leaves have fallen, these trees look as though they have been uprooted and stuck back in the ground upside down!

Right. *It is important to understand the plight of the native agriculturists. This gentleman is probably wearing his best and only shorts. Under the pressure of human population growth and the growing awareness of better lives enjoyed elsewhere, how can one expect developing nations to be sympathetic to conservation?*

Peasant agriculture is so labor intensive that restriction to small family size is a luxury that tropical agricultural families cannot afford. The failure of birth-control programs in India and Southeast Asia is not due to ignorance on the part of the people, or inability to pay for the devices, but to the necessity for each family to have a sufficiently large number of sons that they are assured of the work force needed to support the family seniors in old age. Human labor is an essential resource that they cannot afford to neglect. Only when dependence on hand labor is reduced can we expect a substantial decline in the growth rate of tropical human populations. Unfortunately, efforts to reduce this dependence are faced with the rising costs of energy to power mechanical substitutes.

Following pages. *By the turn of the century, will all the rain forests of Southeast Asia look like this? Probably. But these terraced rice paddies are only capable of utilizing hand labor, so even with rapid agricultural development there is a trap. The efficient and grand-scale mechanization of temperate agriculture cannot be repeated in the tropics. The soil, topography, and pests are fundamentally different and one cannot transplant temperate principles to the tropics and expect them to work.*

Preceding pages. *This scene at Vara Blanca, Costa Rica, at sixty-five hundred feet (2,000 m), was covered in cloud forest until it was recently cleared for agriculture. Huge areas at similar altitudes elsewhere in Costa Rica are being cleared and planted with tea and coffee.*

Above. *This tablet in Sumatra declares the region to be a forest reserve, but that was in 1932. The forest has gone. Gone for firewood, lumber, and agriculture.*

Right. *This picture of the margin of the highway into Manaus, Amazonas, shows the fate of exposed tropical soil. Notice how each pillar of earth owes its existence only to a capping stone, which protects it from the direct impact of the rain. The topsoil, which was only a few centimeters thick, has long gone. We are witnessing the creation of Amazonian badlands.*

Following pages. *The vegetation may change, but the path of the sun does not. Even when the forests are gone and our recollections are reduced to picture books and slide shows, there will still be magnificent sunsets.*

Endpiece. *The evening sun creates beautiful silhouettes of isolated trees along the banks of the Amazon near Belém. Trees such as these, once part of the rain forest, are a constant reminder of the stature and grandeur of the native forests before "development" by humans.*

Acknowledgments

I am very grateful for the encouragement and help I have received from my many friends in the National Museum of Natural History, Smithsonian Institution. First of all I want to thank my good friend and helper Barbara Bedette for her assistance in making this book. I extend my gratitude to the publishers for their patience and valuable suggestions, particularly to my friends Margaret L. Kaplan and Fritz H. Landshoff. Mention should also be made of Joan E. Fisher for her capable editing. A special thanks to my many helpers in the field who enabled me to photograph plants and animals in rain forests around the world. I am immeasurably grateful to the following people:

Dr. Soernatono Adisoemarto, Lembaga Biologi Nasional, Indonesia; Dr. Edward S. Ayensu, Smithsonian Institution; Dr. Graziela M. Barron, Jardim Botanico do Rio de Janeiro; Drs. Roger and Ookeow Beaver, Chian Mai University, Thailand; Dr. Douglas C. Ferguson, United States Department of Agriculture; Dr. J. Linsley Gressitt, Wau Ecology Institute, New Guinea; Dr. Leo J. Hickey, Smithsonian Institution; Professor Kenneth P. Lamb, University of Papua and New Guinea; Dr. Donald J. Ortner, Smithsonian Institution; Dr. João Murca Pires, IPEAN, Belém, Brazil; Dr. Ivan Polunin, University of Singapore; Judy Rodden Schnedl, Washington, D.C.; Professor Margot Schumm, Montgomery Community College, Maryland; Professor Laura Schuster, Universidad A. de la Selva, Peru; Dr. Alcides R. Teixeira, Instituto de Botanico, São Paulo; Kirsten Wegener-Kofoed, Copenhagen, Denmark; Dr. Thomas R. Waller, Smithsonian Institution; J. S. Womersley, Lae Botanical Gardens, New Guinea; Choo See Yan Brothers, Cameroon Highlands, Malaysia; Professor Fernández Yepez, University of Maracay, Venezuela.

K. S.

The youth who today yearns to be the fastest gun in the West was born a hundred years too late. The incipient Captain Kirk who dreams of piloting his own *Enterprise* to distant constellations was born much, much too soon. I was lucky, I was born just right: a time when legal suits were considered ungentlemanly, youthful minds were not parasitized by television, and driving "ton-up" was not against the law. Later, I was able to witness the closing years of British colonialism and meet and marry my friend Janet. Actuarial tables now predict that I can expect to enjoy tropical biology until both the rain forests   I become recycled at the turn of the century.

Principally, I have my father to thank. Thirty-seven years a bachelor, a widower at 39, and totally unappreciated by his son during his lifetime, at least I can now belatedly say "Thanks, Dad."

M.E.

Selected Bibliography

Ashton, P.S. 1977. A contribution of rain forest research to evolutionary theory. *Annals of the Missouri Botanical Gardens* 64: 694—705.

Baker, H.G. 1975. Sugar concentrations in nectars from hummingbird flowers. *Biotropica* 7 (1): 37—41.

Bates, H.W. 1862. Contributions to an insect fauna of the Amazon Valley, Lepidoptera: Heliconiidae. *Transactions of the Linnaean Society of London* 23: 495—566.

Beard, J.S. 1946. The natural vegetation of Trinidad. *Oxford Forestry Memoirs* 20: 1—152.

Beck, L. 1971. Bodenzoologische Gliederung und Charakterisierung des amazonischen Regenwaldes. *Amazoniana* 3: 36—132.

Belt, T. 1874. *The naturalist in Nicaragua.* London: John Murray.

Brower, L.P., L.M. Cook, and H.J. Croze. 1965. Predator response to artificial Batesian mimics released in a neotropical environment. *Evolution* 21: 11—23.

Bultman, J.D., and C.R. Southwell. 1976. Natural resistance of tropical American woods to terrestrial wood-destroying organisms. *Biotropica* 8 (2): 71—95.

Croat, T.B. 1975. Phenological behavior of habit and habitat classes on Barro Colorado Island. *Biotropica* 7 (4): 270—277.

Denison, W.C. 1973. Life in tall trees. *Scientific American* 228 (6): 74—80.

Downhower, J. 1975. The distribution of ants on *Cecropia* leaves. *Biotropica* 7 (1): 59—62.

Eisenberg, J.F., and R.W. Thorington. 1973. A preliminary analysis of a neotropical mammal fauna. *Biotropica* 5 (3): 150—161.

Fittkau, E.J., and H. Klinge. 1973. On biomass and trophic structure of the central Amazonian rain forest ecosystem. *Biotropica* 5 (1): 2—14.

Goodland, R.J.A., and H.S. Irwin. 1975. *Amazon jungle: green hell to red desert?* New York: Elsevier Scientific.

Gotwald, William H., Jr., 1978. Trophic ecology and adaptation in tropical Old World ants of the subfamily Dorylinae (Hymenoptera: Formicidae). *Biotropica* 10 (3): 161—169.

Hallé, F., R.A.A. Oldeman and P.B. Tomlinson. 1978. *Tropical trees and forests.* New York: Springer-Verlag.

Hardy, F. 1978a. The lack of synchrony in the development of plant formations and soils. *Biotropica* 10 (1): 71—72.

———. 1978b. Soils and natural vegetation in Trinidad, W.I. *Biotropica* 10 (1): 70—71.

Henwood, K. 1973. A structural model of forces in buttressed tropical rain forest trees. *Biotropica* 5 (2): 83—93.

Holdridge, L.R., W.C. Grenke, W.H. Hathaway, T. Liang, and J.A. Tosi, Jr. 1971. *Forest environments in tropical life zones.* Oxford, England: Pergamon Press.

Hölldobler, B. 1971. Communication between ants and their guests. *Scientific American* 244 (3): 86—93.

Janzen, D.H. 1966. Coevolution of mutualism between ants and acacias in Central America. *Evolution* 20: 249—275.

———. 1974a. Epiphytic myrmecophytes in Sarawak: mutualism through the feeding of plants by ants. *Biotropica* 6 (4): 237—259.

———. 1974b. Tropical blackwater rivers, animals, and mast fruiting by the Dipterocarpaceae. *Biotropica* 6 (2): 69—103.

——— *et al.* 1976. Changes in the arthropod community along an elevational transect in the Venezuelan Andes. *Biotropica* 8 (3): 193—203.

Jordan, C.F., F. Golley, Jerry Hall, and Jan Hall. 1979. Nutrient scavenging of rainfall by the canopy of an Amazonian rain forest. *Biotropica.*

Kingdon, J. 1971, 1974, 1978. *East African mammals:* An atlas of evolution in Africa. Vols. I, IIA — IIB, IIIA. New York: Academic Press.

Klopfer, P.H. 1957. An experiment in emphatic learning in ducks. *American Naturalist* 91: 61—63.

Lawick-Goodall, J. Van. 1971. *In the shadow of man.* Boston: Houghton Mifflin.

Lloyd, J.E. 1975. Aggressive mimicry in *Photuris* fireflies: signal repertoire by femmes fatales. *Science* 187: 452—453.

McKey, D. 1979. Interaction of the ant-plant *Leonardoxa africana* (Caesalpinaceae) with its obligate inhabitants in rain forests in Cameroon. *Biotropica.*

———, D., P.G. Waterman, C.N. Mbi, J.S. Gartlan, and T.T. Struhsaker. 1978. Phenolic content of vegetation in two African rain forests: ecological implications. *Science* 202 (4363): 61—64.

Markl, H. 1968. Vibrationssignale als Notalarm bei Blattschneiderameisen. *Zoologischer Anzeiger* 30 (suppl.): 343—351.

Meijer, W. 1973. Devastation and regeneration of lowland dipterocarp forest on Southeast Asia. *BioScience* 23 (9): 528—533.

Mertens, R. 1966. Das Problem der Mimikry bei Korallenschlangen. *Zoologische Jahrbücher (Syst.)* 84: 541—576.

Müller, F. 1878. Veber die Vortheile der Mimikry bei Schmetterlingen. *Zoologischer Anzeiger.* 1: 54—55.

Parley, P. 1839. *Peter Parley's tales of animals.* Louisville, Kentucky: Morton and Griswold.

Perry, D.R. 1978a. Factors affecting arboreal epiphytic phytosochology in Central America. *Biotropica* 10 (3): 235—237.

———. 1978b. A method of access into the crowns of emergent and canopy trees. *Biotropica* 10 (2): 155—157.

Prance, G.T. 1977. Floristic inventory of the tropics. Where do we stand? *Annals of the Missouri Botanical Gardens* 64 (4): 659—684.

Purseglove, J.W. 1968, 1972. *Tropical crops.* Dicotyledons 1 and 2, Monocotyledons 1. New York: Halsted Press.

Richards, P.W. 1952. *The tropical rain forest.* Cambridge, England: Cambridge University Press.

Rockwood, L.L. 1975. The effects of seasonality on foraging in two species of leaf-cutting ants *(Atta)* in Guanacaste Province, Costa Rica. *Biotropica* 7 (3): 176—193.

———. 1976. Plant selection and foraging patterns in two species of leaf-cutting ants. *Ecology* 57: 48—61.

Rowell, T. 1973. *The social behavior of monkeys.* Baltimore: Penguin.

Schimper, A.F.W. 1903. Plant geography upon a physical basis. 2nd edition, edited by P. Groom and I.B. Balfour. English translation by W.R. Fisher. *Oxford.*

Scott, N.J. 1976. The abundance and diversity of the herpetofaunas of tropical forest litter. *Biotropica* 8 (1): 41—58.

Singer, P. 1975. *Animal liberation: a new ethic for our treatment of animals.* New York: Random House.

Sioli, H. 1973. Recent human activities in the Brazilian Amazon region and their ecological effect. *In* Meggers, B.J., E.S. Ayensu, and W.D. Duckworth (Eds.). *Tropical forest ecosystems in Africa and South America: a comparative review.* Washington, D.C.: Smithsonian Institution Press.

Smith, A.P. 1979. Buttressing of tropical trees in relation to bark thickness in Dominica, B.W.I. *Biotropica.*

Smith, S.M. 1975. Innate recognition of coral snake pattern by a possible avian predator. *Science* 187: 759—760.

Stiles, F.G. 1978. Temporal organization of flowering among the hummingbird foodplants of a wet tropical forest. *Biotropica* 10 (3): 194—210.

Suthers, R.A. 1966. Optomotor responses by echolocating bats. *Science* 152: 1,102—1,104.

Terwilliger, V.J. 1978. Natural history of Baird's tapir on Barro Colorado Island, Panama. *Biotropica* 10 (3): 211—220.

Wallace, A.R. 1876. *The geographical distribution of animals.* Vols. I and II. New York: Republished by Hafner Publishing Company, 1962.

Washburn, S.L., and I. DeVore. 1961. The social life of baboons. *Scientific American* 204 (6): 62—71.

Weber, N.A. 1966. Fungus-growing ants. *Science* 153 (3736): 587—604.

Wegener, A.L. 1924. *The origin of continents and oceans.* New York: Methuen and Company.

Whitmore, T.C. 1975. *Tropical rain forests of the Far East.* Oxford, England: Clarendon Press.

Williams, T.C., J.M. Williams, and D.R. Griffin. 1966. The homing ability of the neotropical bat *Phyllostomus hastatus,* with evidence for visual orientation. *Animal Behavior* 14: 468—473.

Wilson, E.O. *The insect societies.* Cambridge, Massachusetts: Belknap Press.

GENERAL READING

Bates, M. 1964. *The land and wildlife of South America.* Life Nature Library. New York: Time-Life.

Carr, A. 1964. *The land and wildlife of Africa.* Life Nature Library. New York: Time-Life.

Farb, P. 1967. *Ecology.* Life Nature Library. New York: Time-Life.

Ripley, S.D. 1964. *The land and wildlife of tropical Asia.* Life Nature Library. New York: Time-Life.

Index

Numbers in italic refer to illustrations

Photograph Credits

All photographs for this book were provided by Kjell B. Sandved except the following: 53 (bottom): Judith Skog; 130: Kenneth W. Fink, Ardea Photographics; 131 (top): Arthur Christiansen, Bruce Coleman, Inc.; 131 (bottom): Liz & Tony Bomford, Ardea Photographics; 132: Kenneth W. Fink, Bruce Coleman, Inc.; 133: Kenneth W. Fink, Ardea Photographics; 178: Wolfgang Bayer, Bruce Coleman, Inc.; 183: M.D. England, Ardea Photographics; 187: Wardene Weisser, Ardea Photographics.